how to feel most excellent!

about who you are
(and really enjoy it)

Spending Prime
Time With God

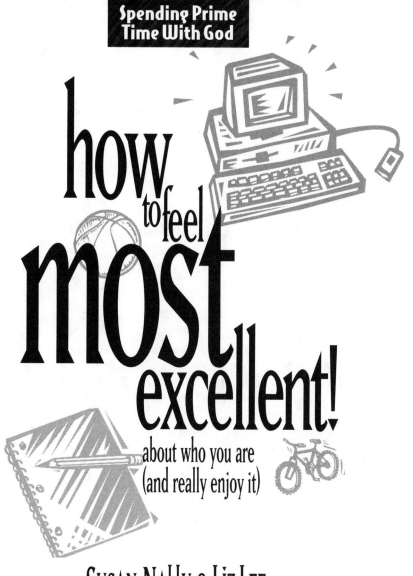

how to feel
most
excellent!

about who you are
(and really enjoy it)

Susan Nally & Liz Lee

Broadman
& Holman
Publishers

Nashville, Tennessee

With grateful appreciation to two very special men
who have been patient, kind, and understanding listeners
during the many months of writing, reading, and editing
of this special work.
Love and thanks to our husbands, Tom and Doug.

Contents

▼

Introduction

▼

Does your life have direction? Would it help to know where you're going? Would you like a map to help?

Knowing God's plan for your life will let you feel "most excellent" about yourself. God wants you to discover His plan for your life, and the Bible is the best place to start. When you know your destination and have a plan (map), you can find your way (God's plan).

This book will lead you to explore what Jesus teaches about life. Jesus maps directions for salvation, prayer, Bible study, worship, giving, trusting the Holy Spirit, treatment of others, forgiveness, helpfulness, care of your body and care of God's world.

There are several key phrases that will guide you. By *Exploring God's Word* you will read and review Bible passages; you will *Evaluate Your Position* by discovering what you think about the information; *Charting Your Course* is a modern day story; *Directing Your Way,* will help you remember what God wants you to do in difficult situations by learning Bible verses; and *Holding Your Course* will give you opportunity to read, write, or think a prayer.

As you begin this journey prepare yourself by gathering a Bible, pencil, ruler, extra paper, highlighter, and several markers.

Now you're ready to start. Ask God to help you finish the journey. It may last twelve weeks or it may take longer. You are the "driver!" You decide how much time you spend on each session. Take your time and enjoy your journey. Your destination is: *How to Feel Most Excellent! About Who You Are (and Really Enjoy It).*

▼

Chapter One

Jesus Teaches You to Be Saved

▼

Vacation time! You've waited so long. Now at last, the day! Perhaps you shouted as you raced out the door, "I've got the front seat first!"

Just as you have a beginning place for a trip, you also have a beginning point for your Christian life. That point is salvation.

When taking a trip, you need certain items. Without a doubt, you must have a map or directions. With your Christian life, you also need a map or directions. It is the Bible. Get yours now!

In this chapter you will use your Bible as a map. You will have an opportunity to sketch, outline, and map your own direction with salvation. Take time to complete each activity.

Directing Your Way:

Below you will find a list of stages which you will pass or have already passed with salvation. They are not in the correct order. As you study each day, you will determine the order. Read and complete each session, and then write the words in the correct order.

acceptance
sharing
lost
forgiveness
sin
conviction
repentance

In the meantime Saul kept up his violent threats of murder against the followers of the Lord. He went to the High Priest.

— Acts 9:1

Friend or Foe?

▼

Exploring God's Word:

Find and read Acts 9:1–3. Saul had grown up with the very best. His father was a Roman citizen and came from the Hebrew line of Benjamin. Saul was very proud of his Jewish background. He had even been named for the first king of Israel.

As a young man, Saul heard that the Jews were being accused of putting to death a man claiming to be the long-awaited Messiah. The man's name was Jesus. Even after His death, a large number of Jews believed Jesus was the promised one, and began meeting together regularly. These followers had even been known to break the Jewish laws. One day Saul was present when one of the "Jesus people" spoke before the Jewish high priest. The man said that Jesus was not dead, but alive. This made the group of high priests so angry that they ordered him to be stoned to death.

Saul watched as the man died. Saul was glad the man was stoned. Saul wanted all of those who followed Jesus to be dead. Saul decided he would help to find those who followed Jesus.

In Acts 9:1–3 underline all of the words that let you know that Saul did not want any part of Jesus or His followers.

4

Charting Your Course:

"Tell your mom and dad we are going to a movie," Janet said to Morgan. "Then we can go to the ice cream place where all of the cute older guys hang out."

"Well, I don't know," Morgan answered. "I really got into trouble the last time we did that. I don't know how they always find out. How come your folks don't care?"

"Oh, they would be mad, but they work late a lot, so they are glad that I find things to do," Janet answered.

"I don't feel right sneaking around and hiding things from my folks," said Morgan. "You know if they find out, they will make us stop being friends."

"So what? I'll just find someone else," Janet answered.

Evaluate Your Position:

What do you know about God? God is _Great, Prince of peace, mighty one._

Think about Janet, and remember what Saul was like. List how Janet and Saul are alike. Janet and Saul are _both like trouble makers and trying to get their own shelf in trouble and their friends_

Holding Your Course:

Dear God,
I am sad when I remember how it feels to be separated from You.
Help me not to allow things I do, things I say, or things I think to come between us. Salvation is a great gift.
I thank You, Lord.
Amen.

▼

[Saul] asked [the High Priest] for letters of introduction to the synagogues in Damascus, so that if he should find there any followers of the Way of the Lord, he would be able to arrest them, both men and women, and bring them back to Jerusalem.

— Acts 9:2

So What!

▼

Exploring God's Word:

To continue the story of Saul, read Acts 9:2–4. Saul went to the court of the high priest. He asked for permission to hunt and kill the Christians. Saul went into their homes and arrested them—putting them in chains and into prison. It seemed the more people Saul was able to find, the more he wanted to find. He was angry. These people accused his race of the murder of the Messiah.

Hurrying along the road to Damascus, Saul held letters from the high priest which gave him the authority to imprison the followers of Jesus. Suddenly a bright light from heaven flashed around Saul. Saul fell to the ground. He knew what he was going to do was wrong.

Charting Your Course:

Morgan was angry. *Mom and Dad are unreasonable,* she thought as she lay across her bed. How dare they say Janet was not a good person for her to have as a friend! So what if Janet didn't always tell her parents where she was going and what she was doing? So what if she flirted with older boys? So what if she talked about Morgan's other friends? So what if she didn't go to church? *So what?* Morgan thought.

It all started when Mom asked Morgan to help by taking care of John Luke for a couple of hours. Morgan said she had other plans. Dad asked what those plans were. Morgan replied, "Janet and I are going to a movie." Mom suggested that Morgan call Janet and invite her over to watch a movie at home. When Morgan called, Janet said, "We weren't *really* going to a movie. We were going to the ice cream store. Tell your folks you don't want to stay with John Luke."

That's when Mom and Dad really got steamed. *And now I'm stuck here!* Morgan thought.

As Morgan lay there thinking, she remembered something her Sunday School teacher said. "Boys and girls, when you know something is wrong and do it anyway, the Bible says that is sin."

Sin, sin, sin! The word seemed to echo in Morgan's head.

Evaluate Your Position:

Everyone has sinned and is far away from God's saving presence.

— Romans 3:23

Sin separates you from right relationships. A word that describes the awareness of sin's presence, and the need for God in our lives is *conviction.* Conviction is knowing that God wants you to have the best relationships, and that He will help you. Conviction is recognizing your sin. Think about how you felt when you did something wrong. How did you realize your actions, thoughts, or attitudes were wrong? Write down some things that can separate you from a right relationship with God on a journal page (in the back of the book).

Holding Your Course:

Lord, I am sad when I do things that make people mad at me.
Sometimes I don't know why I do them.
Thank You for reminding me of these wrongs.
Thank You for wanting me to be Yours.
Amen.

▼

*He fell to the ground and heard a voice saying to him, "Saul, Saul!
Why do you persecute me?" "Who are you, Lord?" [Saul] asked. "I am
Jesus, whom you persecute," the voice said.*

— Acts 9:4–5

What a Mess!

▼

Exploring God's Word:

As the horses' hooves beat against the road, a light suddenly flashed
around Saul. He fell to the road. The voice spoke to Saul in the
Hebrew language. Saul could not look up. He was afraid. What Saul
wanted to do to those who believed in Jesus was wrong.

"I am Jesus, the very one you are persecuting. Stand up," the voice
said.

Getting to his knees, Saul tried to stand. He tried to look up, but
the light was too bright. Covering his eyes with his hands, Saul stood
up.

"What do you want of me?" Saul asked.

The voice answered, "Go to Damascus. There you will be told
what to do next."

Saul could not see. He was led to Damascus.

Charting Your Course:

(If you have not done so, read the story in day 2 in this chapter before
reading this story.) Morgan lay very still. It was as if a voice was saying
to her, "Morgan, you know your parents are right about Janet. She is

not a good influence. She encourages you to do things you know are not right. When you know something is wrong and do it anyway, it is sin."

Morgan got up. As she stood looking out of the window, she remembered hearing that Jesus loves every individual, but He hates sin. Sin separates Jesus from the individual.

"That is why I have acted so unkind. That is why I have not felt good about Janet but couldn't seem to stand up to her," Morgan said out loud. "I have wanted to do only what I wanted. I have not cared about anyone but me. Oh, what a mess!"

Morgan really felt sorry for all the hurt she had caused. She hurt Jesus. She hurt herself. She hurt her family. There by herself, standing by the window, she said, "Jesus, I am so very sorry."

Evaluate Your Position:

Often as you travel in a vehicle, you will hit bumps or "dips"—ones that may even cause the vehicle to break or stop operating. Sin is like that. Sin can cause relationships to break or stop operating.

Each vehicle listed below needs an essential part. The parts are listed. Match each part with a vehicle. On the line beside the part write an action, a thought, or an attitude you have that separates you from a good relationship with Jesus.

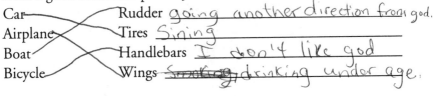

Car   Rudder _going another direction from god._
Airplane   Tires _Sining_
Boat   Handlebars _I don't like god_
Bicycle   Wings _~~smoking~~ drinking under age._

Holding Your Course:

Dear God,
I feel bad when I think about all I have done to hurt myself and others.
Most of all I feel sad when I think how I have hurt You, Jesus.
I am so very sorry.
Amen.

▼

So Ananias went, entered the house where Saul was, and placed his hands on him. "Brother Saul," he said, "the Lord has sent me—Jesus himself, who appeared to you on the road as you were coming here. He sent me so that you might see again and be filled with the Holy Spirit."

— Acts 9:17

I'm Sorry

▼

Exploring God's Word:

Saul did not see anything for three days. He did not eat or drink anything for three days. Many, many times he must have thought about all that had happened. How sad Saul must have felt, knowing so many people were in prison because of him. What strange happenings—the voice from heaven, the light flashing all around, Saul remembered it all very well.

Thinking about all he had heard and seen, Saul realized he must also surrender his life to Jesus. Saul himself would now be one of the very ones whom he had been trying to put into prison.

Charting Your Course:

When Morgan admitted she had allowed Janet to influence her to do things that were wrong, she felt very sorry. Morgan told Jesus how sorry she was for doing things she knew were wrong. The anger she felt toward her parents really was anger at herself. As Morgan began talking out loud to Jesus, other things she had done came to mind. Morgan told Jesus she was sorry for those also. As Morgan talked, the out-of-sorts, angry feelings she had began to leave.

"Jesus," Morgan said, "I don't like being separated from You. I am sorry. I want You to take my life, my thoughts, and my will and control them. You be in control instead of me. I am trusting You for Your forgiveness. Amen."

Evaluate Your Position:

Sin must not be your master;
for you do not live under law but under God's grace.

— Romans 6:14

Surrendering is a hard thing to do, because we all like to be in control. To surrender is to give up, to release, to relinquish. As you journey through life, there are many times when you must surrender. If Jesus is in control of your life, you have Him to guide you. In the space below list attitudes, thoughts, and actions that you need to surrender.

ATTITUDES	THOUGHTS	ACTIONS
Have good Attitudes		let god direct me,

Holding Your Course:

I feel peace, Lord, when I surrender my will to You.
I get into the most trouble when I don't allow You to control my life.
Thank You for forgiving me.
I do trust You.
Amen.

▼

At once something like fish scales fell from Saul's eyes, and he was able to see again. He stood up and was baptized; and after he had eaten, his strength came back.

— Acts 9:18–19

The Change

▼

Exploring God's Word:

Saul did not eat or drink for three days. He had not been able to see for three days. Then a man named Ananias went to the house where Saul was. It was hard for Ananias to go because he knew why Saul had come to Damascus. He was afraid Saul would arrest him.

What a surprise for Ananias to find Saul at the house—blind and weak from lack of food.

"Jesus, the voice that spoke to you on the road, has sent me to you," Ananias said. "I was afraid to come, but Jesus said you are to be His chosen instrument to tell others about Him."

Immediately, Saul could see. He was hungry and he ate.

"I want to be baptized," Saul said.

Charting Your Course:

Morgan ran downstairs. Just as she reached the bottom of the stairs, she stopped. Suddenly she was afraid. Would Mom and Dad accept her apology? Would they believe she now knew Janet had not been a good friend? How would she tell them that she had asked Jesus to forgive her and to take control of her life? Just then, Mother called out, "Morgan, is that you? Are you over your pouting?"

Slowly Morgan walked into the room.

"Why, Morgan!" Dad exclaimed, "You're smiling. What have you been doing?"

"I have something to tell you," Morgan began. "I am not the same Morgan who went into my room." Morgan began telling what had happened. She told them about asking Jesus to forgive her and to take control of her life. She told them she was sorry for hurting them.

"I want to be baptized," Morgan told her parents.

Evaluate Your Position:

It's not enough just to know your destination on a journey, you must also know how to get there—the road numbers, the miles, whether you must spend a night, etc. The same is true in life. When you ask Jesus to take control, you must do His will, not yours. You must obey.

Below you will find some verses to help you know how to obey Him. Find them in your Bible and unscramble the word(s). Learn one of the verses to help you remember what God wants you to do.

Deuteronomy 6:18   ghtri and oogd   _right and good_
Psalm 4:3   eahrs   _hears_
Psalm 55:16–17   allc (rpya)   _call_
Psalm 86:5   rogifev   _forgive_
Proverbs 3:5–6   rutst   _trust_
Proverbs 8:7   peask rutth   _speak   truth_
Ephesians 6:1   beyo entspar   _obey   parents_
1 John 4:11   ovle neo onathre   _love one another_

Holding Your Course:

I do want to obey You, God. I know You can help me.
Thank You for giving me the Bible
to help me to know what You want me to do.
Amen.

▼

Ananias answered, "Lord, many people have told me about this man and about all the terrible things he has done to your people in Jerusalem. And he has come to Damascus with authority from the chief priests to arrest all who worship you." The Lord said to him, "Go, because I have chosen him to serve me."

— Acts 9:13–15

Should I Tell?

▼

Exploring God's Word:

Ananias had to do something really hard—to do what the Lord told him to do, Ananias had to have trust and faith. "Do I have to?" Ananias was saying.

To ask Jesus to control your life is one thing, but to follow Him in what He tells and teaches is another, and it is not always easy. Ananias realized that when God told him to go to Saul. It took all of the courage Ananias possessed. He now had to put into practice obeying God.

What thoughts Ananias must have had as he walked the dusty streets to the house of Judas. How slowly he must have walked.

Charting Your Course:

It had not been easy since Morgan had asked Jesus to control her life. She was trying to obey His teaching, but she did not find obeying to be easy. Janet was her best friend. Morgan thought Janet would not be her friend if she knew. So far Morgan had been able to have a real excuse when Janet wanted to sneak away to the ice cream shop to see the guys, but...

14

At breakfast one morning, Dad read Matthew 10:32–33. "Whoever acknowledges me before men, I will also acknowledge him before my Father in heaven. But whoever disowns me before men, I will disown him before my Father in heaven" (NIV).

All day Morgan thought about the verse. She knew she had to tell Janet about Jesus. How would Janet treat her then? Morgan's heart beat fast every time she saw Janet.

As they were leaving school, Morgan said, "Janet, I have some exciting news to tell you."

Evaluate Your Position:

Have you ever needed directions for getting someplace? Telling someone about Jesus is like giving directions. Only those who have been to a place can give directions on how to get there. You are telling them "firsthand" the way to go. You are a witness to the way. You have been there.

To help you in giving directions to someone about Jesus, complete the sentences below.

Before I knew Jesus, I was _____

_____

I realized I needed Jesus when I _____

_____

I accepted Jesus by _____

_____

Jesus helped me today by _____

_____

Holding Your Course:

I don't know why I can talk about the movie I saw, the game I won,
or my favorite food, but I can't talk about You, Lord. I am sorry.
Help me to tell someone what I have written down.
Amen.

▼

He went straight to the synagogues and began to preach that Jesus was the Son of God.

— Acts 9:20

The Good Friend

▼

Exploring God's Word:

What happened on that road changed Saul forever. He met Jesus. Instead of hunting the believers, he became one of them. Just as eagerly as Saul sought out the believers to punish them, he now preached about Jesus. What a change! The Jews did not like the change in Saul. They decided to kill him. God warned Saul and he escaped to Jerusalem.

In Jerusalem, Saul went to join Jesus' disciples. They were afraid of Saul. They thought it was a trick. Barnabas stood and told of Saul's experience. He told how God had spoken to Saul. He told them Saul had changed. Because Barnabas trusted Saul, the others did too. Barnabas was a good friend.

Charting Your Course:

Janet sat quietly as Morgan told her about asking Jesus to take control of her life. Softly, Janet said, "I have really felt lousy about slipping around. Oh, Morgan, I am sorry. I have not only done wrong, but I have asked you to do wrong with me. Tell me what to do."

Morgan opened her Bible.

Evaluate Your Position:

Mark these verses in your Bible to help you direct a friend to Jesus.

1. Find Acts 4:13. At the top of the page write "Lost=aware of a great need for God." Turn to the first page of your Bible and write "Turn to page _____" (write the page number of Acts 4:13).

2. Find Acts 3:19. At the top of the page write: "Sin=sorry for wrong thoughts, attitudes, behaviors. Go back to Acts 4:13." At the bottom of the page write "Turn to page _____" (write the page number of Acts 3:19).

3. Find Romans 10:9. At the top of the page write "Trusting God for His forgiveness—giving Him control of my life." Go back to Acts 3:19. At the bottom of the page, write "Turn to page ____" (write the page number of Romans 10:9).

4. Find 1 John 1:9. At the top of the page write "Pardoned and saved from my sins by accepting God's mercy and love." Go back to Romans 10:9. At the bottom of the page write "Turn to page____" (write the page number of 1 John 1:9).

5. Find Ephesians 2:10. At the top of the page write "Doing God's will and obeying His teachings." Go back to 1 John 1:9. At the bottom of the page write "Turn to page ____" (write the page number of Ephesians 2:10).

6. At the bottom of the page of Ephesians 2:10 write "Prayer, See last page of Bible." On the last page, write a prayer like this example: "Dear Jesus, I am sorry for sin that separates us. I do not want sin to be a part of my life any longer. Forgive me. I accept the forgiveness You give. I give You my life and will. I want to obey You. Amen."

Holding Your Course:

Dear God,
thank You for being my friend and for giving Your only Son to die for
my sin. Help me be a good friend to others by telling them about You.
Amen.

▼

Chapter Two

Jesus Teaches
You to Pray

▼

Life is like a journey. On a journey, it is fun to have someone go with you to talk to and to share with.

After you ask Jesus to take control of your life and to be your Lord and Savior, He wants you to talk to Him. The word that often is used for talking to Jesus is *prayer*.

In this chapter you may relate to the characters in each story. You may want to talk to God about your feelings. You may want to talk to God about your actions. As you read this chapter you will discover times and ways to talk to God.

Be ready to explore your own course as you discover when and how to talk to God. You will want to keep a prayer log each day. You will need your Bible, a pen or pencil, and paper for the prayer log. In the log you will record your daily events. You will identify those things you want to talk (pray) about. Then you will write your prayer(s).

As you think about prayer, remember the following:

▲ Prayer is personal—only you can tell God what you want to tell Him.

▲ Prayer is private—the words and thoughts you tell God are yours even when you pray out loud with others or others pray out loud in your presence.

▲ Prayer has purpose—talking to God lets you involve Him in all that you do.

▲ Prayer is fellowship and love—which God wants most.

Begin now talking to God about every happening of your day. Include and involve God in all that you do, say, and think.

*After Jesus finished saying this, he looked up to heaven and said,
"Father, the hour has come. Give glory to your Son, so that the Son
may give glory to you. For you gave him authority over all mankind,
so that he might give eternal life to all those you gave him. And eternal
life means to know you, the only true God, and to know Jesus Christ,
whom you sent. I have shown your glory on earth; I have finished the
work you gave me to do."*

— John 17:1–4

A Hard Thing to Do

▼

Exploring God's Word:

As you read the Bible passage in your Bible, underline the name Jesus
called God. Why do you think we call God "Father"? When you ask
Him to be your Savior, He becomes your Father God.

In John 17:1–4, draw a box around the phrase that tells you what
Jesus wants the people to know about God. Draw an uneven line
under the word that means to worship and praise or to give glory to.
(Clue: G_o_y.) How many times did you find the word? _____. Jesus
wanted God to approve of what He was doing. Jesus showed respect
to God.

Jesus knew there were those who wanted to kill Him. Jesus had
been sent by God to tell all who would listen and believe about God.
Now even the church people were mad at Jesus. Jesus may have felt
as though everyone was against Him. Have you ever felt that way?
Jesus prayed first for Himself. You can too.

Charting Your Course:

Jared's friend had AIDS! Jared had spent the night with Robert the
night before Robert went to the doctor.

Jared sat quietly as his parents explained that Robert was very sick. They assured Jared that he could not catch AIDS just from spending the night. They wanted Jared to still be friends with Robert. They wanted Jared to help Robert with others who would not understand his illness. What they asked Jared to do was hard.

At first Jared was angry. Why did his best friend have to be sick? Then he felt very sad. Maybe it was all a mistake. How could he face his other friends? Would they think he might have it? Would they think he could give it to them? Jared's thoughts whirled in his head.

Suddenly he remembered something his Dad had said, "Always remember, Jared, you now have a Father God who cares about everything you do, say, hear, or see. You can tell Him anything and everything. You just talk to Him. It is called praying."

Jared lay across his bed. He began telling God all the things he was feeling and thinking. He even told God how angry he was that Robert was sick. He told God that it would be hard being Robert's friend. Jared asked God to help him. Jared felt better knowing he had talked to God. He wanted to tell Robert to talk to God too. Jared rode his bike to Robert's house. He knew God would help them both do what they had to do. It would be hard.

Evaluate Your Position:

In your prayer log write a prayer Jared may say. Write a prayer for Robert. Write one for yourself. Remember to put the date at the top of the page in your prayer log each time you make an entry.

Holding Your Course:

Prayer is telling God the hard things you have to do. You do not need certain words. You just talk!

Dear God,
help me to do the hard things.
Help me to make You a part of everything I say and do.
Amen

▼

"I pray for them. I do not pray for the world but for those you gave me, for they belong to you. All I have is yours, and all you have is mine; and my glory is shown through them."

— John 17:9–10

The Surprise Friend

▼

Exploring God's Word:

The religious leaders hated Jesus because He told them He was God's Son. The religious leaders wanted Him dead. Jesus knew He was hated. Jesus was ready and willing to do God's will, but death on a cross would be a very painful death. And Jesus knew the day was coming soon.

He wanted to help His friends to be prepared. Jesus talked to them about what was going to happen, but they didn't understand. So Jesus prayed. He talked to God about Himself and God's plan for Him. He then talked to God about His friends.

Find John 17:6–10 and underline the phrases that tell:

▲ How Jesus got His friends.
▲ What the friends know about God.
▲ Who the friends really belong to.
▲ What Jesus received because of His friends.

Charting Your Course:

Carol's mom called the family for dinner. As Carol came running into the room, she stopped. There on the table at her place was a large box wrapped in the prettiest paper and ribbon she'd ever seen. As she slowly walked to her place, the whole family was looking at her and smiling.

"What is it? Who gave it to me?" Carol asked, as she tore into the package.

As she lifted the lid, she yelled, "Wow, look at this! It is the dress I've been saving my money for. Where did it come from? What did I do to get it?" Carol squealed.

"Slow down," Mom said. "Mrs. Rogers sent it. She said you were a big help to her while her broken ankle was healing. She wanted to do something to tell you how much your being her friend meant to her. She brought the dress over to surprise you."

Carol sat quietly hugging the dress to herself. "I've been saving so long. This is really a surprise. I'll call and thank her!" Carol said.

"Carol," Mrs. Rogers said on the telephone, "It is fun to surprise you. You have been so good to me. I didn't know what I would do when I came home from the hospital. All of my family lives far away. You never complained because you were not able to play with your friends while you helped care for me. I am so thankful that you are my friend."

Evaluate Your Position:

In your prayer log write a prayer Carol might say. Write a prayer for Mrs. Rogers. Remember: put today's date on your page.

Holding Your Course:

Dear God,
thank You for friends.
I am so glad You have given me friends who care about me.
Help me to be a good friend too.
Amen.

▼

"And now I am coming to you; I am no longer in the world, but they are in the world. Holy Father! Keep them safe by the power of your name, the name you gave me, so that they may be one just as you and I are one. While I was with them, I kept them safe by the power of your name, the name you gave me. I protected them, and not one of them was lost, except the man who was bound to be lost—so that the scripture might come true."

— John 17:11–12

Betrayed

Exploring God's Word:

How difficult it must have been for Jesus to know He would be leaving His friends. The disciples had been with Him nearly three years. Some were fishermen, one a tax collector, one a writer, and another a scholar. All left what they were doing and stopped their careers to follow Jesus. Jesus loved these men.

In John 17:11–12, underline what Jesus knew would happen to Him. Circle what Jesus asked God to do for His friends.

One of Jesus' friends would change. He would betray (turn against) Jesus. How very disappointed Jesus must have been with Judas. Yet Jesus knew even the betrayal was part of God's plan for salvation.

Charting Your Course:

It was the last inning of the playoffs. The two teams were from the same town. The winning team would be the state champ.

Henry stepped up to bat. He had hit two home runs, but so had the other team. Now the score was tied. Henry was nervous, but he thought, *I can do it.*

The first ball was called, "Ball one!"

Henry swung hard at the next two balls.

Calm down, Henry thought. *That is Philip, my friend, pitching. He and I practice together all of the time. I always hit his pitches. I can this time too.*

"Ball two!" the umpire shouted.

Then the ball came fast toward Henry. It was a good pitch. Henry struck hard.

"Strike three, you're out!" the umpire shouted.

Henry just stood there. He could not believe he had missed. With disbelief he watched as the other side went wild. They were the champs. Henry's team had lost. Henry felt betrayed.

Henry's family tried to cheer him up, but he felt too sad. He knew he missed the ball, but Philip was his friend.

"It's Philip on the phone for you," Henry's mom said.

How could he, Henry thought. *He is the one who struck me out. He cost my team the championship. Some friend!*

"Tell him I don't want to talk," Henry told his mom.

When his mom returned to the room, she said, "I am disappointed in you. Philip is your friend. What would you have done if you had been in Philip's place?"

Evaluate Your Position:

In your prayer log write a prayer Henry might say. Write a prayer for Philip. Remember to write the date.

Praying is not always easy to do. When unpleasant things occur or we don't win, we get angry with God. We stop talking to Him.

Holding Your Course:

Dear God,
sometimes I don't treat You well. I get mad and don't talk to You.
I blame You for what happens to me.
I need to put myself in Your place and think about Your feelings.
Please help me to think of You.
Amen.

▼

"I do not ask you to take them out of the world, but I do ask you to keep them safe from the Evil One. Just as I do not belong to the world, they do not belong to the world. Dedicate them to yourself by means of the truth; your word is truth. I sent them into the world, just as you sent me into the world."

— John 17:15–18

My Fault?

▼

Exploring God's Word:

Jesus knew that in death He would soon be going to be with God, and that thought brought Him joy. He wanted the disciples to know that death meant life with God.

In John 17:13–19, underline the words that tell what Jesus gave to the disciples that the world hated. Draw a circle around the verse that tells Jesus' prayer for these He loved. Put dotted lines under the phrase that tells what "truth" is. Write the word "Bible" near the phrase.

It would have been easy for Jesus to ask God to take the disciples to heaven with Him, but He did not.

Jesus knew His disciples would need protection. He knew it would not be easy for them to live up to God's purposes. History reports the disciples eventually were put to death because of their belief in God. Peter was crucified and John beheaded because they would not stop telling that Jesus was alive.

Go back and read all of Jesus' prayer for His disciples, John 17:6–19. Read the passage out loud and try to imagine how Jesus felt as He talked to God.

Charting Your Course:

Mom and Dad were fighting again. Robin covered her ears with her hands. She did not want to listen, but their voices came through, loud. Suddenly a door slammed. All was quiet. After a time, Robin went out the back door to her friend's house.

Missy listened as Robin told her what happened. Missy got a washcloth for Robin to wash her eyes. Missy hugged Robin.

"I don't know why they fight," Robin said, crying again. "I wonder if I'm the reason. They were upset with my report card, but I worked hard. I thought when I asked Jesus to take control of my life everything would be great, but it didn't even stop their fighting."

"Robin," Missy said, "I found a verse you need to hear. Jesus must have felt somewhat like you. People wanted Him dead. There was much fighting and arguing about Him. Just before He knew He was to die, He prayed for His friends. Jesus said something like this, 'I know, God, that You can't take My friends out of the world, and that the world won't always be a pleasant place to live, but take care of them as they live during the rough times.'"

"His parents weren't fighting!" Robin said.

"No," Missy answered, "He is reminding us that even when things aren't easy, God is with us. We are not alone!"

Evaluate Your Position:

In your prayer log write a prayer Robin could pray. Write a prayer for Missy. Remember: the date.

Holding Your Course:

Dear God,
living and getting along with people is hard. I don't understand why
those I love so much do not show love for each other.
I often feel hurt. Please help me.
Amen.

▼

"I pray not only for them, but also for those who believe in me because of their message. I pray that they may all be one. Father! May they be in us, just as you are in me and I am in you. May they be one, so that the world will believe that you sent me."

— John 17:20–21

A Gift for Remembering

▼

Exploring God's Word:

It helps to get a special gift when someone you love has to leave. The gift can remind you of them. It can help you tell others about them. Jesus gave such a gift. He gave eternal life through trust in God. Jesus wants people who have received the gift to tell others. His prayer was that each person who knows God will tell someone else about Him. With your Bible open to John 17:20–26, complete the following:

▲ Jesus' prayer was for us to be o_____.

▲ Jesus and God are o_____.

▲ Jesus wanted future believers to know that God l_____ them.

▲ Jesus knew that God l_____ Him.

▲ Jesus wanted the world to k_____ God.

▲ Jesus said the world would k___ God because they k___ Him.

▲ Jesus said when we l_____ and a_____ Him as our Lord, we a_____ and l_____ God.

Charting Your Course:

Aunt Mary was visiting! Vicki and Jenny loved Aunt Mary. She was a missionary in Africa. One night, she told them this story.

"Once," she said, "I was teaching the women how to cook more nutritionally. We were outside, gathered around a large pot of water boiling on the fire. Three poles held the pot above the fire, and one of the village women accidentally hit one of the sticks. The pot tilted, spilling the hot water on another woman's leg. Quickly the other women helped me carry her to a nearby stream. We laid her in the cool water, and the woman stopped screaming.

"By then most of the village had gathered. Most of the villagers did not believe in God. The lady who was burned was a Christian. As she lay in the stream, she began to pray. Everyone got very quiet. They listened.

"After many weeks the lady began to heal. Because the lady prayed, many in the village asked to know God.

"Jennifer and Vicki, I want you to pray for me. I want you to pray for the village people. My work is hard. It helps me very much to know that you pray for me," Aunt Mary finished.

Much too soon, it was time to take Aunt Mary to the airport. They would not see her for several years. Just before she got on the airplane, she gave each of the girls a small clay pot. "The people of the village make large ones like these to sell," Aunt Mary told the girls. "Keep it where you can see it to remind you of me."

Evaluate Your Position:

In your prayer log, write a prayer that Jennifer and Vicki might say. Write a prayer Aunt Mary would say. Remember to put today's date at the top of your page.

Holding Your Course:

Dear God, it is hard to talk to You when I do not see You.
Then someone I love and trust talks about You
or does something to help me know about You.
Thank You for people who help me to know You are real.
Amen.

▼

"Father! You have given them to me,
and I want them to be with me where I am,
so that they may see my glory, the glory you gave me;
for you loved me before the world was made."
— John 17:24

A True Friend

▼

Exploring God's Word:

Jesus wanted His followers to be powerful witnesses of God. Jesus asked God to help these men to see God's glory in Him. Then, because His followers remembered Him, they would pray for each other. What a special trust Jesus was asking God for! Jesus was saying, "Father, because I love these so much, help them to see You in Me. Help them to love each other with Your same love. Please keep them caring of each other. Help them not to argue or fight with each other." In John 17:24, underline the phrase that tells how long God loved Jesus.

Charting Your Course:

Amy and Donna were practicing for cheerleading tryouts. Amy jumped high. As she came down, she landed hard. She heard a popping sound. Then pain shot through her leg.

"Oh, oh, I hurt my leg," said Amy. She began to cry. Donna ran for help.

Later that night as Amy lay propped in bed, Donna said, "I'm so sorry this happened. I was counting on us being cheerleaders together.

Now you won't be well in time for the tryouts. It is just not fair!" Donna flung herself on the chair beside the bed.

A tear rolled down Amy's cheek as she said, "I am so disappointed. The doctor said I would be in this cast for six weeks. No, it's not fair. I wanted this so much."

Donna went to the bed and gave Amy a hug. "Don't cry. I am going to pray every night that you will get well quicker. After all, tryouts are still five weeks away."

Weeks passed. Every day Donna went to see Amy. Amy did not seem to be making much progress. Every day Donna prayed.

The day after tryouts, Donna slowly entered Amy's room.

"Well, tell me quick, did you make it?" Amy asked.

Sadly, Donna looked at Amy. "Yes, I did, but it's no fun, knowing that you wanted to be a cheerleader too. I am not sure I'll keep it because I always wanted to be your partner. Besides, I'm really mad at that stuff they told us in church. You know, about asking God for something important and He would always give it to you. I don't believe that stuff anymore after this!"

"No," Amy said, "I want you to be a cheerleader. I'm happy for you. Our practice paid off. I'll yell the loudest for you. I'm disappointed, but God is helping me not to have pain with my leg. I'll be your partner in the bleachers. You'll cheer for us both."

Donna hugged Amy. "You're a true friend," Donna said.

Evaluating Your Position:

In your prayer log, write a prayer that Amy may have said. Write one that Donna said.

Holding Your Course:

Dear God,
I am sorry that I treat You like someone who can give me everything I want. I am glad that You give me what I need. Thank You.
Amen.

▼

"I made you known to them, and I will continue to do so, in order that the love you have for me may be in them, and so that I also may be in them."

— John 17:26

My Confidant

▼

Exploring God's Word:

In this chapter you've had the opportunity to begin a lifelong habit of talking to God about everything. Jesus knew you would not have an easy time living with others. He also knew you would be tempted. Jesus prayed: "Father, I have lived on earth to prove that You are real. I have told them of Your great love, and I am willing to die for them. Now Father, will You continue to make Yourself known by letting them know that I, Jesus, will be in them. Those who accept You can talk to Me, for I will always be with them" (John 17:24–26, paraphrased). Jesus lives within you when you accept Him as your Savior. He becomes your partner, your helper, and your confidant (someone to share your secret thoughts, hopes, desires, attitudes, and feelings).

Prayer is your way of talking to God. Jesus will not force His help or care on you. Prayer is asking and allowing God to do His best for you. We are responsible for seeking His best—that is prayer.

Charting Your Course:

Find and read Luke 11:1–13. These verses contain the prayer that Jesus taught to His disciples as an example of how to pray (vv. 2–4).

If you still feel uncomfortable praying, use it as your model to think of what to say. Write your own prayer on one of the journal pages in the back of this book using this model prayer as your guide.

Bible Prayer	My Prayer
Father:...	[person talking to]
May your name be honored..................	[expression of respect]
May your kingdom come	[recognition of deity]
Give us day by day the food we need.....	[request for daily help]
Forgive us our sins, for we forgive everyone who does us wrong	[acknowledge sin, ask for forgiveness, forgive others]
And do not bring us to hard testing.	[request help against temptation]

(End the conversation)

Prayer (conversation) with God becomes natural when you realize that He is real. God wants you to talk to Him. He is your very best friend and confidant.

Evaluate Your Position:

Continue to keep your prayer log. Write a prayer each day in your log. Notice how you become aware of God's help.

Holding Your Course:

Dear God,
I am so glad that You are able to hear me at any time and at any place. I often think about how great You are.
Help me to forgive others like You forgive me.
Help me this day to let You control my life.
Help me to do what is right.
Thank You for being my best friend and confidant.
Amen.

▼

Chapter Three

Jesus Teaches
You to Study

▼

Have you ever said, "I hate to study"? If you're like most, you probably have. It often seems unnecessary. This week you will learn how Jesus studied and prepared Himself to do what God wanted. This week's work may help you to like studying a little better and to understand why it is important.

Think about the meaning of the word *study*: "the process one goes through to try to learn something." You might have to read, think, question, or discuss with someone else to understand a particular subject. Studying may involve one or all of these actions.

Evaluate Your Position:

Make a graph showing your behavior, attitudes, and feelings about studying. Place a dot at the appropriate place on the graph to show how you feel or act concerning each statement below (0, lowest; 10, highest). A=study habits, B=place where you study, C=results of your study, D=feelings when you study, E=how you feel about studying.

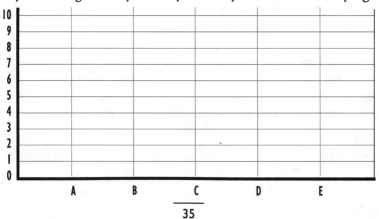

On the third day they found him in the Temple, sitting with the Jewish teachers, listening to them and asking questions. All who heard him were amazed at his intelligent answers. His parents were astonished when they saw him.

— Luke 2:46—48

What Is Study?
▼

Exploring God's Word:

In Luke 2:41–52, you find the story of Jesus' visit to the temple as a twelve-year-old boy. Take time to read this passage before you go further in this lesson.

▲ His parents began retracing their steps to Jerusalem. How long did it take them to find Jesus?_____

▲ What was Jesus doing? _____

▲ Verse 47 tells us that all that heard Him were_____

▲ In verse 48 we learn that Jesus' parents were _____

▲ What question did Jesus' mother ask Him? _____

The last part of verse 48 tells us how worried Jesus' parents were about His disappearance. Unfortunately, they did not understand Jesus' need to be in the temple questioning, listening, and talking to the Jewish teachers of the day. Jesus was studying and learning.

It's important for us to know that because Jesus had learned His lessons well as a young boy, and because His mother and father had taught Him at home, He was prepared to talk with the leaders in the temple. Even though Jesus was God's Son while He was on earth, He was also human. Jesus faithfully prepared for His earthly ministry, just as each one of us must faithfully prepare for our life's work.

Charting Your Course:

How would you finish this story to reflect the results of your Bible study? Use the lines below to tell the rest of the story.

Spring was Billy's favorite time of year. Billy played both soccer and baseball. It was great fun having something to do every afternoon after school. He spent lots of time with his friends during practice and games. Every Saturday he had at least one game and usually two.

Billy's teachers noticed that most mornings he came in dragging his book bag and acting tired. It wasn't long before Billy's parents got a call from one of his teachers. To his parents' surprise, the teacher told them that Billy hadn't turned in completed assignments in over two weeks.

When Billy arrived home from practice, _____

_____

_____

_____

_____

_____

_____

_____

_____

_____

Holding Your Course:

Dear God,
it's so easy to get involved in too many things.
Please help me to know how to choose wisely the extra things I do.
Also help me to spend my study time wisely,
so that You will be proud of the work that I do.
Amen.

▼

On the third day they found him in the Temple, sitting with the Jewish teachers, listening to them and asking questions. All who heard him were amazed at his intelligent answers.

— Luke 2:46–47

Study Is Discipline!

▼

Exploring God's Word:

Look again at Luke 2:41–52 to discover how important it is for you to discipline yourself to study. The word *discipline* means "training." A disciplined person has an orderly and controlled behavior.

▲ What did you discover about Jesus? Find verse 46 again. Who was with Jesus in the temple? _____

▲ What was Jesus doing? _____

▲ Verse 47 says that all that heard Him were _____

Age	Kind of School	What He Studied
6–10	Synagogue	memorized Scripture
10–15	oral interpretation	listened to & studied Scripture
13	"Son of the Law"	read from Books of the Law & became member of the synagogue congregation
20+	Synagogue	Each Monday, Thursday & feast and fast days.

Because Jesus learned His lessons, He was able to understand and participate in the discussions in the temple. Study the chart on the previous page to learn about Jesus' education.

Jesus spent His time wisely as He studied God's Word. By controlling His behavior, Jesus was able to memorize Scripture that would help Him all the days of His life.

Charting Your Course:

Finish this story to reflect the Bible study above.

Jonathan was a very good student. He had just completed the fifth grade. Jonathan's mom received a call from the guidance counselor at school. She wanted the family to come for a conference the next day. During the discussion at dinner that night, Jonathan looked a little puzzled when his mom told him he had to go, too.

When Jonathan and his parents arrived, the counselor was ready for the Smiths. Mr. and Mrs. Smith went into her office. She asked Jonathan to wait in the outer office.

The counselor complimented the Smiths on Jonathan's good grades and high scores. She felt that this indicated that Jonathan had good study habits. She wanted the Smiths to consider placing Jonathan in the accelerated program.

Jonathan _____

_____

_____

_____

_____

Holding Your Course:

Dear God,
please help me to "train myself" or discipline myself so that I can be
better prepared when I study.
Amen.

▼

On the third day they found him in the Temple, sitting with the Jewish teachers, listening to them and asking questions.

— Luke 2:46

Ways You Study

▼

Exploring God's Word:

Reread Luke 2:46. Notice that Jesus was doing two things that were helpful—He was listening and He was asking questions. What are some things that you do that help you to study (learn)?

Unscramble the words below.

1. a d e r _____   5. e n e i x m a _____
2. s c d i s u s _____   6. y p a p l _____
3. k h n t i _____   7. n l e t i s _____
4. n t q i e u s o _____   8. u t d n e s r n ad _____

Have you thought about doing these things as a part of studying? You know that when you read you are studying. It is also helpful to discuss and ask questions—friends, parents, and teachers are great resources.

When you listen to what others are saying, it helps you understand. Taking time to examine and think about what you are studying is helpful. After doing these things, you will be able to apply what you've learned. On the next graph, show how you use each of these eight things (0, lowest; 10, highest). A=read, B=think, C=examine, D=listen, E=discuss, F=question, G=apply, H=understand.

Jesus learned to do all of these things so that He would be prepared to face the challenges that were ahead. You do not know what challenges lie ahead of you, so prepare yourself well!

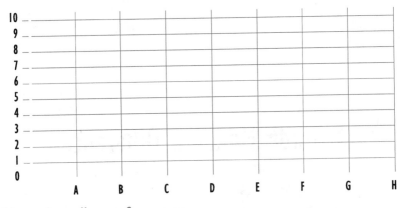

Charting Your Course:

The tape player is running as Joey listens to the message from his teacher. Joey has a broken leg. Mrs. Jones sends Joey's assignments home to him every day. He must keep his leg raised and stay in bed for three weeks. He's glad he doesn't have to go to school like this. Problem: Joey doesn't want to get behind in his work. There's less than two months of school left. Joey wants to graduate and go to the new middle school with all his friends.

Finish the story by telling how Joey can use the eight things from the graph to help him with his studying.

Holding Your Course:

Dear God,
I must confess that I really don't like to study.
Although I like to make good grades, it's often difficult to concentrate.
Help me to remember each of the eight things from this study
so I will be better prepared.
Amen.

▼

He answered them, "Why did you have to look for me? Didn't you know that I had to be in my Father's house?" But they did not understand his answer.

— Luke 2:49–50

Attitude Makes a Difference!

▼

Exploring God's Word:

Read Luke 2:48–50 to find the answers to the following questions.

▲ What question did Jesus' mother ask Him? _____

_____

▲ In verse 48 Mary told Jesus how she and Joseph felt. What was her statement? _____

_____

▲ Jesus was surprised that His parents were worried. What words in verse 49 show that surprise? _____

_____

Jesus didn't mean to worry His parents. He didn't mean to make them return to Jerusalem to look for Him. Jesus was so caught up in talking with the teachers that He forgot all else.

Have you ever been so involved in studying that you forgot all else? Jesus' attitude about learning made the difference. Today, think of how Jesus' attitudes affected His studying and the results of His studying.

Evaluate Your Position:

An attitude is a way of thinking about something. What kind of an attitude do you have? To receive positive results from studying, you must have a "willing attitude." Tell in your own words what you think is meant by a "willing attitude." Tell how you think your attitude affects your studying. _____

_____

_____

_____

_____

Charting Your Course:

Use today's Bible study to help you finish the following story. Use the lines below.

Phil and Tommy decided to work together on their history project. The boys wanted to make a large salt map to represent their country. The assignment had five parts that had to be coverered before the project would be completed.

As the boys began to make their plans, Phil could see there was going to be a problem. Tommy didn't want to do his share of the work. Phil wanted to make an "A" on this project, so he knew how important it was for the two of them to get along. Phil decided to:

_____

_____

_____

_____

Holding Your Course:

Dear God,
I know that my attitude affects how I think about studying.
Help me to improve my attitude, so that I can always do my best.
Amen.

▼

When the festival was over...the boy Jesus stayed in Jerusalem. His parents did not know this; they thought that he was with the group, so they traveled a whole day and then started looking for him among their relatives and friends.

— Luke 2:43–44

Pay Attention to Details!

▼

Exploring God's Word:

Look closely at the details in verses 41–45 of Luke 2.

▲ Why was the family traveling to Jerusalem ? _____

_____

▲ What was Jesus' age ? _____

▲ What does verse 43 tell you happened to Jesus? _____

_____

▲ How long was it before His parents realized Jesus was missing ?

_____

▲ Where did His parents look? _____

▲ What did Jesus' parents do when they couldn't find Him? _____

_____

This passage is interesting. Parents today would hardly go a whole day before they realized a child was missing from their traveling group. But remember, this group of many families was traveling at a slow pace compared to modern travel, and the children of these families often played together in a group of their own. The fact that a son was missing was not a small detail.

Evaluate Your Position:

Think about how paying attention to details affects what happens. Have you heard the saying "Don't sweat the small stuff"? "Small stuff" could be the details involved in finishing a project or paper. What about checking to make sure you have crossed all your t's, dotted your i's, or checked to make sure all your punctuation is correct? Maybe one of the details you need to check is how neatly your work is presented. List other "small stuff" details on one of the journal pages.

Charting Your Course:

As a result of today's Bible study, how would you finish this story?

Mrs. Jones is Tim's English teacher. She is very particular about the work that is turned in to her. At the beginning of the year Mrs. Jones lectured the class, saying that papers had to be headed a certain way, they had to be neat, and they could have no careless mistakes.

Tim hates to go back over his work after he has finished it. He doesn't think he should have to clean up his work just to suit Mrs. Jones. The semester is almost over. Tim wants to impress Mrs. Jones with how much he has learned. One problem! Tim forgets to pay attention to the "small stuff." Tell about the assignment Tim turns in and what happens.

_____

_____

_____

_____

Holding Your Course:

Dear God,
as much as I hate to admit it, I know that the "small stuff" is
important in everything that I do.
Please help me to treat it that way.
Amen.

▼

He answered them, "Why did you have to look for me? Didn't you know that I had to be in my Father's house?" But they did not understand his answer.

So Jesus went back with them to Nazareth, where he was obedient to them. His mother treasured all these things in her heart.

— Luke 2:49–51

Study Brings Understanding

▼

Exploring God's Word:

Verses 49–52 of Luke 2 show a lack of understanding on the part of Jesus' parents. What two questions did Jesus ask His parents?

▲ _____

▲ _____

Jesus' parents didn't understand what Jesus was saying to them. Their lack of understanding didn't keep Jesus from obeying them. Jesus returned to _____ and Mary kept all that happened in her heart. The word *understanding* means to grasp the meaning of something. Did you "understand" that by studying and preparing Himself, Jesus understood what God wanted Him to do? Did you also see why Jesus' parents did not understand what was happening? They had not spent the time and energy necessary to come to an understanding of what Jesus was doing.

What is it you need to do in order to come to an understanding of something you need to learn? Make a "to do" list on the lines below.

_____

_____

_____

Evaluate Your Position:

Think how each of the things you've listed will help you better understand what you are studying. Talk to a parent about what you are having trouble understanding. Decide together what could be done to help you improve your level of understanding. You might be surprised at what happens between you and your parent because of this sharing.

Charting Your Course:

As a result of your Bible study, how would you finish this story?

Suzie has always had a hard time in math. She never saw a reason why she had to do things a certain way. Many times Suzie would skip a step or simply try to do it her own way, always resulting in a wrong answer. The worst part was Suzie didn't understand the way the teacher explained things. Most days she only half listened to the explanations. Suzie's mistakes were always the teacher's fault.

No one at home helped Suzie with her math. Her sister was always on the phone and Mom always seemed busy. Homework assignments were impossible and almost always brought tears. Suzie never realized she could help herself.

What needs to be done?

_____

_____

_____

_____

_____

Holding Your Course:

Dear God,
I get very frustrated when I don't understand what I am studying.
Help me to study harder, so that I will better understand.
Amen.

▼

Jesus grew both in both body and in wisdom, gaining favor with God and men.

— Luke 2:52

Benefits

▼

Exploring God's Word:

As you begin today, reread the entire passage of Luke 2:41–52. Pay close attention to the last verse. List the three ways that Jesus grew.

▲ _____

▲ _____

▲ _____

The first way Jesus grew was in body. This means that he grew physically. Eating properly and getting enough sleep and exercise affects your physical growth. The second way Jesus grew was in wisdom. This means that He was gaining knowledge. What affects how much knowledge you gain?

Thirdly, Jesus grew in favor with both God and men. The word *favor* in this verse means that He gained approval. Name some of the ways you have learned that Jesus gained approval.

_____   _____

_____   _____

Gaining approval from both God and men is a benefit. A benefit is something that helps a person. Do you receive any benefits from studying?

_____

Evaluate Your Position:

Think about what you want to gain approval for. List four things on the left side. On the right side, tell what benefits you will receive.

1. _____   _____
2. _____   _____
3. _____   _____
4. _____   _____

Charting Your Course:

As a result of your Bible study in this chapter, you will tell your own story. You are the main character. You need to include information that will show how you will be able to benefit from what you have learned. When you finish writing, reread your story, paying close attention to details. Then make corrections and share your story with a parent or friend. (If you need more room, use your own paper and keep it in your book).

_____
_____
_____
_____
_____
_____

Holding Your Course:

Dear God,
help me remember that the benefits far outweigh the work it takes
to do my best when studying.
Thank You for providing me with a good mind and the ability to
remember what I study.
Help me make learning enjoyable.
Amen.

▼

Chapter Four

Jesus Teaches You to Learn His Word

▼

Think about the different Scripture verses that you can recite from memory. Do they ever come to mind when you have a decision to make? Think about how knowing Scripture can often help you know what to do in difficult situations. Use the space below to list any Scriptures that are meaningful to you.

_____   _____
_____   _____
_____   _____
_____   _____

In this chapter we will discover how knowing Scripture helped Jesus respond when He was tempted. Our Bible passage is found in the first book of the New Testament. Find Matthew 4:1–10. Take a few minutes to read through the passage. Underline the three ways Jesus was tempted. Put a star by the way Jesus answered the temptation.

Holding Your Course:

On the lines below write a prayer asking God to help you learn Scriptures that will help you face the difficult times we all encounter.

_____
_____
_____
_____
_____

Then the Devil came to him and said, "If you are God's Son, order these stones to turn into bread."…and… "If you are God's Son, throw yourself down, for the scripture says, 'God will give orders to his angels about you; they will hold you up with their hands, so that not even your feet will be hurt on the stones.'" …"All this I will give you," the Devil said, "if you kneel down and worship me."

— Matthew 4:3, 6, 9

A Problem

▼

Exploring God's Word:

Three times in Matthew 4:1–10 the devil tries to tempt Jesus by presenting Him with a choice. The first two choices are of a personal and social nature.

The first temptation: Jesus was hungry after spending forty days in the desert. He also knew that He could feed the hungry people of the world if He did what the devil suggested. Jesus wanted hungry people to know that they need more than this kind of food.

The second temptation: True faith does not expect God to answer with amazing acts. If Jesus had chosen to take a "leap of faith," He would have been trying to force God into taking a certain action. Jesus knew that He should not test God. As amazing as this would have been, the excitement would not have lasted. The people would have been no closer to knowing and trusting God.

The third temptation: This time, the devil changes directions. He tempts Jesus with political power. Would "gaining the world," as the devil suggests, be worth bowing down to the devil? Another way to think about this is that this would be, "selling yourself" for the price of obeying the devil.

Evaluate Your Position:

Each of the temptations was designed to help Jesus achieve a quick, self-centered goal at the expense of His reason for being in this world. Think about why you are in this world. Watch your step!

Charting Your Course:

Football season is an exciting time for Johnny. He had spent several years on a junior pro team. Now it is time to play with the older boys.

On the first day of practice, Johnny woke up and got dressed early. He could hardly wait. Mom hurriedly fixed his breakfast. "Hey, Dad, come on let's go!" he yelled.

As Johnny and his dad walked onto the field, some of the guys on the team began to whisper. Johnny tried not to notice. As soon as his dad began to talk to the other fathers, one of them called Johnny. "What's your name?" he demanded. It only took a few minutes for Johnny to realize that these guys were "tough." They told him what they expected of him. They also quickly let him know that this was not something the coaches knew about. Johnny just nodded.

After a two-hour practice, the coach called the team to the center of the field. He handed out copies of the team rules. As they walked off the field, Johnny heard one guy tell him to slow up. Johnny didn't want to wait. He was afraid! More than anything Johnny wanted to play football, but he also knew how important it was to follow the rules.

Holding Your Course:

Dear Lord,
sometimes it is hard to give up something I really want
when I know it would be so much fun.
Like Johnny, I find that some of my choices are hard.
Help me to know what You want me to do and make the right choices.
Amen.

▼

Then the Spirit led Jesus into the desert to be tempted by the Devil.
After spending forty days and nights without food, Jesus was hungry.
— Matthew 4:1–2

The Rules

▼

Exploring God's Word:

Jesus had just been baptized when He went off into the desert to be alone with His heavenly Father. He was planning to spend this time fasting and meditating while He was preparing Himself for His earthly ministry. Unfortunately the devil had other ideas.

Think about how you feel when you are hungry. Your hunger probably starts after only a few hours. How long had Jesus gone without food? _____ Imagine how He must have felt. Do you think He was tired and weak. How do you think you would feel if you went that long without food? _____

_____

The word *tempted* in this passage means that Jesus was tested by the devil. Stop and think again about Jesus' physical condition. The devil probably thought that he would be able to trick Jesus into sinning because of His weakened state.

Evaluate Your Position:

Think about how you might be tempted. A popular saying a few years ago was, "The devil made me do it!" Many times when it was said it sounded like an excuse for doing what was wrong. Remember Jesus' physical condition. Are you ever in a weakened condition when you are tempted? On the lines below write about a time when you were tempted.

_____

_____

_____

Charting Your Course:

As Johnny jumped in the car he yelled, "Let's get out of here, quick!" Dad looked surprised but said nothing. When they were almost home Johnny said, "Promise you won't tell." Johnny didn't wait for an answer. "Dad, I need your help. Those guys scare me." Surprised, Dad asked, "Would you like to tell me why?"

Johnny was trying hard not to cry. "Those guys told me that I would have to follow their rules if I wanted to be a part of their team. They really frightened me. I'm not sure what they meant by 'their rules.'" Johnny continued, "I'm afraid I'll get hurt or that something bad will happen if I listen to them." Johnny's dad wanted to know exactly what the other boys had said. When Johnny finished he explained that it wasn't so much what they said, but how they looked at him. Johnny said he felt threatened.

"Dad, I want to play football, but I don't think I can play if I'm expected to follow two sets of rules," Johnny confessed. He didn't want to give up football. He knew his dad would help him with this problem. He was glad he could share it with him.

Holding Your Course:

Lord,
help me to be strong even at times when I am tempted.
Help me to remember my body is Yours.
Amen.

▼

Then the Devil came to him and said, "If you are God's Son, order these stones to turn into bread." ... and ... "If you are God's Son, throw yourself down, for the scripture says, 'God will give orders to his angels about you; they will hold you up with their hands, so that not even your feet will be hurt on the stones.'"... "All this I will give you," the Devil said, "if you kneel down and worship me."

— Matthew 4:3, 6, 9

Sinful Opportunities

▼

Exploring God's Word:

Today we will look again at Matthew 4:3, 6, 9. Each of these verses shows a sinful opportunity when Jesus was tempted by the devil. Temptation by itself is not sin; it is an *opportunity* to sin. Although Jesus chose not to participate, the opportunity was present. If He had chosen to give in to what the devil suggested, He would have sinned.

Sin is giving in to these "sinful opportunities." Each temptation Jesus experienced was mixed with good. That made it harder for Jesus. The devil is good at deception, but Jesus knew that He could not accomplish God's purpose by using the devil's methods.

Evaluate Your Position:

Are there opportunities for you to sin? Of course! We all are tempted. Remember that temptation is not sin, but our response to temptation could become sin. On the "warning signs" to the left, write three temptations you face that are "sinful opportunities" that could become sin.

Charting Your Course:

Johnny and his dad finally arrived home. Johnny was really tired. Dad suggested a quick shower.

While in the shower Johnny began to think about what happened. Just a couple of hours ago, he had been so excited about playing. Football was important to Johnny, but Johnny had never been a "snitch." *What am I going to do? Who will I follow?*

The team rules were laying on Johnny's bed when he got out of the shower. He sat down and began to read them. He wondered about the other "rules" hinted at by the guy on the team. Dad walked into his room, sat down beside Johnny, and asked, "Feeling any better?"

"Dad, maybe I ought to do what the guys said. Do you think it would be all right to try it awhile, and then decide?" Dad understood Johnny's confusion. "I think it would only make the decision harder if you wait. I'm sure that what they're suggesting is against the team rules. If it weren't, then why would they warn you not to let the coach know?" Dad asked patiently.

Johnny and his dad continued to talk. Dad told Johnny that he was proud of him for coming to him with this problem. "This won't be the last time you will be faced with a tough decision," Dad told him. "Football is fun and it is a good sport. There will always be temptations to play by different rules. It's when we choose to make our own rules that trouble happens."

Holding Your Course:

Lord,
sometimes life is so unfair and I am confused about what I should do.
Help me to remember that You will always show me what's right.
Amen.

▼

But Jesus answered, "The scripture says, 'Man cannot live on bread alone, but needs every word that God speaks.'"

— Matthew 4:4

Defense

▼

Exploring God's Word:

Think back to Jesus' circumstances in Matthew 4:1–10. Before this temptation took place, Jesus had been in the desert. He had been fasting (going without food) and meditating (praying and listening).

Jesus knew better than anyone the Word of God, and it's interesting to note that He didn't get into a discussion of any kind with the devil. Jesus simply quoted a Scripture passage from the Old Testament Book of Deuteronomy.

The devil wanted Jesus to perform a miracle just to satisfy a physical need. Yes, Jesus was hungry. Jesus also knew that man needed more than bread to live. Jesus' reply tells the devil that man needs the Word of God more than bread. Does that mean that Jesus thought that man could live without bread? Probably not. Remember the devil was testing Jesus. Jesus put up a strong defense. This was a defense that the devil could not fight.

Evaluate Your Position:

Look back at your first warning sign in the last session. What temptation did you list? How did you deal with that temptation? If

you haven't dealt with it yet, do it now. What Scripture might help? Ask God to help you withstand the temptation. Write your thoughts below.

_____

_____

Charting Your Course:

It's not easy to take a stand. Johnny was really having a hard time with what was happening. How could he decide what to do? He'd already talked with Dad. Maybe if he talked to his friend, Joe, it would help.

Johnny soon realized he had to make his own decision. Life was really a "bummer" for Johnny right now.

Just before bedtime, Johnny's dad came by his room and suggested that he pray about his problem. "Dad, how can God help me with this? God never played on a football team. How could he understand?" Dad smiled and reminded Johnny that God was able to help with any problem. "It couldn't hurt," responded Johnny.

Johnny picked up his Bible and began to look for a familiar passage, but found nothing. Johnny closed his Bible and then closed his eyes. He sat quietly for a few minutes not saying anything. As he began to pray, a Bible verse came to mind. "Thou shalt do that which is right and good in the sight of the Lord." Once again as he began to pray, he remembered something his Sunday School teacher said about obeying God rather than man. Then Johnny prayed,

Dear Lord,
I really want to play football, but I know I can't play on this team
because of what those guys expect me to do.
Help me to be strong and help me with my disappointment.
Thank You for Your Word that guides my choices.
Amen.

Holding Your Course:

Do you need to pray Johnny's prayer?

Jesus answered, "But the scripture also says, 'Do not put the Lord your God to the test.'"

— Matthew 4:7

Test?

▼

Exploring God's Word:

In Matthew 4:7, Jesus responded to the devil's challenge. What was Jesus' answer?

The devil was suggesting that Jesus do something spectacular in order to prove who He was. Jesus knew better than to do what was being suggested. Can you imagine Jesus throwing Himself down from the highest point of the temple? It almost sounds ridiculous to even think such a thing. What would it accomplish?

In trying to convince Jesus, the devil misused Scripture. He quoted a passage from Psalm 91:11–12. The devil wanted Jesus to take a reckless chance to see if God would protect Him. Jesus knew that this would defeat the purpose of God's plan for His life.

This temptation was also a test of wills. This was a real battle (struggle) between the devil's will and God's will for Jesus' life. Do you think the devil tempts people today in this same way?

Evaluate Your Position:

Look back at your three temptations on the warning signs in day 3. Are any of the temptations a "test of wills"? At this warning sign,

 pause a moment. Think of how this temptation is a test of wills for you. What Scripture could help you make the right response to the test? Write your response below.

_____

_____

Charting Your Course:

Just when Johnny thought he had it all figured out, he got a late-night phone call. The voice on the other end of the phone line was unfamiliar. As Johnny listened his eyes grew bigger from the shock at what was being said. It only took a few minutes for Johnny to get really scared. His only response was, "Sure, I understand." Johnny dropped the receiver like it was a hot potato, as he called to his dad.

The next few minutes helped both Johnny and his dad know that Johnny was really being tested by these guys. "Dad, what should I have said?" His dad reassured him that he had done the right thing.

Decision time had arrived. Johnny didn't understand why this was happening, but he really didn't want to be a part of it. "Dad, I want to call the coach and tell him I am not going to be on the team." Johnny's dad looked at him for a few seconds and then asked, "What reason will you give him when he asks you why?" Both Johnny and his dad sat on the edge of Johnny's bed and realized the problem. Johnny didn't want to lie to the coach, but he didn't want to make the guys mad either. Johnny was afraid of what they might do to him.

Holding Your Course:

Lord,
sometimes the choices I have are hard. I know it is important to be
honest, but sometimes being honest can cause more trouble.
Show me Your way, Lord.
Amen.

▼

Then Jesus answered, "Go away, Satan! The scripture says, 'Worship the Lord your God and serve only him!'"

— Matthew 4:10

Shortcuts!

▼

Exploring God's Word:

This last temptation was different. It presented Jesus with a choice between two masters. Jesus had no trouble choosing.

This time, the devil offered Jesus a shortcut to glory and power. Remember Jesus was about to begin His earthly ministry. There would be other times Jesus would have to choose between popular expectations and obedience to the will of God. Jesus was not only choosing God's will, but also which road He would travel.

Jesus knew that kneeling down and worshiping the devil would not gain Him the whole world. This was the only temptation that involved anything that was immoral. For Jesus or anyone else to worship Satan would be sinful. Satan used this temptation to offer Jesus a deal. This temptation shows that the devil didn't try to hide his desire for control over Jesus. Satan angered Jesus in this temptation, and Jesus didn't hesitate to tell Satan to "Go away!"

Evaluate Your Position:

Look again at your warning signs in this chapter. Do any of your temptations represent anything that is immoral? (*Immoral* means something that is wicked or evil.) If so, then what choice do you have? Often in temptations the choice to do what is right is many times harder than doing wrong. Stop here. Pray. Ask God to help you with your temptations.

Charting Your Course:

Before Johnny and his dad called the coach, they decided to pray together. Dad listened as Johnny prayed. He felt how hard this was for Johnny. When Johnny finished, his dad gave him a big hug.

Johnny was really nervous as he dialed the coach's number. After he identified himself, he said that he didn't want to be on the team. The coach's only answer was, "Oh!" Johnny sat holding the receiver for what seemed a long time. Then the coach said, "May I ask you a question?" Johnny answered, "I guess so." The coach asked Johnny if he had had a problem with any of the guys on the team. Johnny felt very uncomfortable. Even though he had talked this over with his dad, he was still afraid. "Not, really, sir. I just don't think I belong on this team, and I'm not happy being on it." The coach thanked Johnny for calling and then asked to speak to his dad.

After several minutes Johnny's dad thanked the coach and hung up the phone. "Well, what was he saying?" asked Johnny.

"Seems like these guys have scared not only you, but several of the other new guys as well. The coach has had several other boys call to quit."

Johnny looked surprised. "I didn't know that!"

Dad smiled at Johnny. "The team has a meeting tomorrow and we're both expected to attend."

Holding Your Course:

Thank You, God, for the guidance that I find in Your Word.
It does help me to know what to do.
Amen.

▼

"Go away, Satan!"...Then the Devil left Jesus.
— Matthew 4:10–11

Action Plan

▼

Exploring God's Word:

Temptation is real. Each of us faces temptation every day. This Bible passage teaches us that we can overcome temptations in our life. Each of us has power to send Satan away.

Jesus used Scripture to respond to temptation. Have you discovered that Scripture is a powerful "weapon"? It can only be used if you have studied and learned the importance of the words for your life. Jesus spent many hours meditating and praying. This time that He spent helped Him face His temptations and not give into them. Jesus was sure of what God wanted for His life, so He was able to send the devil away and know that he would go.

List the three temptations in Matthew 4:3,6,9. _____
_____
_____

Now look at the Scriptures that Jesus used to respond to Satan found in Matthew 4:4,7,10. Write what you've learned. _____
_____
_____
_____

Evaluate Your Position:

Scripture is a powerful weapon. Have you armed yourself with this weapon? Take a few minutes to think about the Scriptures you already know that would help you resist temptation. How can you learn more verses that would benefit you? Read over the following plan of action.

Plan of Action:

▲ Look up memory verses in my Bible and underline them.

▲ Write down all verses and their reference in notebook.

▲ In my notebook, highlight or circle with a bright marker all verses that I have memorized and understand.

▲ When I discover a helpful verse, add it to my notebook.

▲ Keep my notebook near my Bible.

▲ Decorate the cover of my notebook.

▲ Find a way to show that I understand what the verses mean. Record how the verses helped me.

▲ Share the verses with a parent or friend after I've learned them.

Charting Your Course:

Listed below are some Scriptures that will help you resist temptation. Begin your notebook now. Use the plan of action. Arm yourself well!

Proverbs 17:17	Galatians 6:10	Isaiah 41:10
Luke 6:3	Ephesians 6:1	John 14:15
Acts 5:29	John 3:16	Acts 10:38

Holding Your Course:

Lord,
help me to "keep your law in my heart,
so that I will not sin against you."
Amen.
[See Psalm 119:11.]

▼

Chapter Five

Jesus Teaches You to Worship

▼

What is worship? Worship is a personal and private experience. No one can force you to worship. To worship God is to express praise for and to God through actions, thoughts, and feelings. Praising God is showing Him honor. The result of worship is serving Him.

The word *worship* is from an old English word *worthship*. Knowing who God is allows you to recognize that He is worthy of our worship. As you experience worship you will:

▲ Experience the presence of the Holy Spirit.
▲ Express adoration and praise to God.
▲ Recognize sins in your life and confess them.
▲ Reaffirm your commitment to serve Jesus Christ.
▲ Renew your spirit to live life daily.

As you study, you will investigate these worship experiences. You will also examine ways to make worship more meaningful. In the following acrostic, write a word relating to worship that begins or contains that letter.

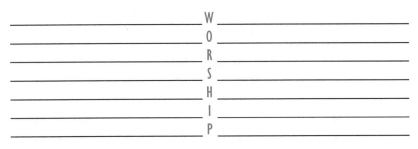

W
O
R
S
H
I
P

I was glad when they said to me, "Let us go to the Lord's house."
— Psalm 122:1

The Night Before

▼

It was Saturday evening, and Jared was excited. Tomorrow he would sit with his friends during church. Several months before, Jared had asked his parents if he could sit with his friends. Sitting together as a family had always been special. Jared's mom and dad talked about how good it made them feel to have the family together during worship. Jared had held the song book for his parents since he was four years old. He had watched as his mom pointed to the words in the Bible even before he could read. His Dad let him help pass the offering plate when it was Dad's turn to be an usher. Jared had loved being with his family, but now he wanted to be with his friends.

Jared carefully laid the clothes for church on the chair beside his bed. He put his Bible and Sunday School book on his dresser near the door. Jared stood looking and thinking. He wanted to be sure he had everything ready. Jared felt good about going to church.

Next door in the Evins house, they were watching TV. They would go to church the next day, but no preparation was being made. Jeremy was usually late to Sunday School. He often grumbled that church is no fun and would never bring his Bible or book.

Exploring God's Word:

This section will help you study worship experiences from the Old Testament (your heritage) and the New Testament (your example).

In Bible times, worship usually took place according to some sort of schedule and/or calendar. Is worship like that today? In Bible times, worship provided religious education and a time of fellowship. How is that true today? Christians have a rich heritage of worship.

Old Testament (heritage): "The Lord God made clothes out of animal skins for Adam and his wife, and he clothed them" (Genesis 3:21).

Sin caused God to turn Adam and Eve out of their garden home. They were not prepared to live outside the garden. God killed an animal to make clothes for them. The animal became a sacrifice for them. This first worship was needed as a result of sin.

New Testament (example): "Every year the parents of Jesus went to Jerusalem for the Passover Festival. When Jesus was twelve years old, they went to the festival as usual" (Luke 2:41–42).

The trip to the temple required several days of walking. The trip was long and slow. The journey required careful preparation. Surely Jesus had duties for helping with the preparation. How excited he must have been to help with the clothes, food, and water for the trip.

Evaluate Your Position:

What was the difference between Jared and Jeremy's feelings about worship? _____

_____

Holding Your Course:

Lord,
I realize the way I prepare for worship makes a difference
in the way I feel about worship. Help me to prepare well.
Amen.

▼
___

"God is Spirit, and only by the power of his Spirit can people worship him as he really is."

— John 4:24

A Special Feeling

▼

Charting Your Course:

Jared bounced up and down in the back seat of the car. He and his family were going to church.

"Jared," Dad said, "put your seat belt on and calm down!"

"I'm excited," Jared answered. "I'm going to sit with my friends!"

"Just remember what we told you," his mom said.

During church, one of Jared's friends began to whisper. Jared put a finger to his lips to tell him to be quiet. Pastor Tom was telling how God proved His presence to the people of Israel and how He showed Himself to Jacob in a dream. He told Jacob He would help him.

Jared was thinking how great it would be if God would prove Himself like that to him. Jared noticed how quiet everyone was. He look around. The building was filled with people listening to Pastor Tom talk about God, and it helped Jared to know God was with him. Jared remembered his teacher talking about Jesus loving His friends so much that He told them after He died that the Holy Spirit would be with them to remind them of Him. His teacher had said, "As you worship, you will be reminded by the Holy Spirit of Jesus' presence." Jared had a special feeling at church.

Exploring God's Word:

Perhaps you have been asked, "Why do you go to church?" or "Why worship?" Worship is the feeling of wanting to be with God.

Old Testament (heritage): "Jacob left Beersheba and started toward Haran. At sunset he came to a holy place and camped there. He lay down to sleep, resting his head on a stone. He dreamed that he saw a stairway reaching from earth to heaven, with angels going up and coming down on it. And there was the Lord standing beside him. 'I am the Lord, the God of Abraham and Isaac,' he said. 'I will give to you and to your descendants this land on which you are lying…Remember, I will be with you and protect you wherever you go'" (Genesis 28:10–13, 15).

Jacob was "on the run." He had tricked his father. He had cheated his brother Esau out of his blessing. Esau wanted to kill Jacob. Even on the run, God let Jacob know that He was with him.

New Testament (example): "I will ask the Father, and he will give you another Helper, who will stay with you forever. He is the Spirit, who reveals the truth about God." (John 14:16–17).

Jesus loved His disciples, and knew they would miss Him. He also knew that Christians in years to come would need help. God gave us the Holy Spirit. You experience the presence of the Holy Spirit in worship, and through His presence, you know that Jesus is real.

Evaluate Your Position:

How do you know God is real. How did Jared "feel God's presence"? Write your answer here: _____

_____

Holding Your Course:

Lord,
thank You for the good feelings I have when I know You are with me.
Amen.

▼
___

For my gladness comes from him.
— Psalm 104:3

The Best Hero

▼

As the sixth graders came into their Sunday School room, they stopped. Pencils, sheets of paper, and pieces of heavy cardboard were scattered on the floor.

"Come in," Mrs. Lee said. "Go to a piece of cardboard with paper and pencil. No talking. Wait for the instructions."

Slowly the children entered the room. As soon as they were seated, Mrs. Lee said, "On the top of your paper, I want you to write the name of the person you most admire, the person who means the most to you, the one who you want to be most like. Next I want you to write words you think describe the person. Last I want you to write words that describe your feelings about that person."

When the children finished writing, Mrs. Lee asked them to sit near her. She then told the story of Mary pouring expensive oil on Jesus' feet and then wiping them with her hair. She worshiped Jesus.

"Now, look at your paper," Mrs. Lee said. "Think about the person that you wrote down. How was Mary's choice better than yours? Why? One by one, the children realized that people today are not people worthy of worship. Only God is worthy of worship.

Taking their church's order of worship bulletin, the class talked about what they could do during their service in order to worship God. They realized that each item was an opportunity to worship. (Do the same with your order of worship.)

Exploring God's Word:

Do you have a hero? What qualities does that person have that you like? Worship should create a desire to be like God. Worship takes place as you recognize the realness of God and His presence with you.

Old Testament (heritage): "The pillar of cloud was always in front of the people during the day, and the pillar of fire at night" (Exodus 13:22).

The Jewish people followed God's instructions to go to the land He promised them. They knew where to go because God lead them with special lights. The Scripture also says that God gave them a movable worship place. It was called the tabernacle. Instructions were given in how to build and use the tabernacle. God's presence was shown by a cloud. From then on, when the cloud lifted from the tent, the people knew it was time to travel. Otherwise they stayed. The cloud of the Lord was over the tabernacle by day, and the fire was in the cloud at night. The people always knew that God was with them.

New Testament (example): "Then Mary took a whole pint of a very expensive perfume made of pure nard, poured it on Jesus' feet, and wiped them with her hair. The sweet smell of the perfume filled the whole house" (John 12:3).

Jesus knew His time on earth was short. He went to the home of a family He loved. Mary did a bold thing. Women were not usually allowed with the men at a meal. Mary recognized Jesus as God's Son.

Holding Your Course:

Lord,
thank You for being with me in a real way.
Amen.

▼

73

But if we confess our sins to God, he will keep his promise and do what is right.

— I John 1:9

Left Out

Charting Your Course:

Erin and Andrea whispered and giggled as they waited for the church service to begin. They were best friends. They were talking about their new school classes. Several benches ahead of them sat Sue Kung. She was in their Sunday School class. She lived near them. Many times Sue sat next to Erin or Andrea in Sunday School. Sue had often invited them to her house to play video games. The girls had never gone. Sue tried to be their friend.

The organ music began. Andrea and Erin stopped talking.

As the service continued, Erin happened to notice Sue. *She sure looks sad,* thought Erin.

Pastor Sam was saying that an offering to God might be the way in which we treat others. Andrea was half listening. Suddenly, she heard the pastor say, "Many people are lonesome, even though there are plenty of others around. As Christians, we should be willing to include others in our friendships."

Erin looked again at Sue and felt very sad.

During the invitation, the pastor said, "Perhaps some of you need to ask God to forgive you for not including others." Erin and Andrea realized they had been selfish not to include Sue. As the invitation hymn was being sung both girls asked for forgiveness.

After church they said at the same time, "Let's see if Sue can come over today." Laughingly they headed toward Sue.

Exploring God's Word:

From the beginning of time people have realized that worship and sin do not mix.

Old Testament (heritage): "When Aaron had finished all the sacrifices, he raised his hands over the people and blessed them, and then stepped down" (Leviticus 9:22).

The Book of Leviticus describes in great detail the offerings that are to be made and why. In Bible times, the family gathered around an altar to worship. Animals were placed on the altar as a sacrifice to God. The altar sacrifice caused the people to recognize sin, to observe the holiness of God, and to seek forgiveness. Later the people built the tabernacle. The individual family altars were done away with. The people gathered at the tabernacle for one sacrifice. With the building of the temple in Jerusalem, the sacrifices were offered by the priests at the great altar in the holy place. The offerings followed an order: forgiveness of sin, dedication, fellowship.

New Testament (example): "Do this in memory of me" (Luke 22:19).

When Jesus came, He removed the need for animal sacrifices. He became the sacrifice for sin. Jesus knew those He loved would need to be reminded of sin. Before Jesus was crucified, He gathered His disciples with Him in a room. Jesus broke bread and served wine. He told them the bread represented His body and the wine, His blood. They were to remember His sacrifice for their sins. Today, this observance is called the Lord's Supper.

Holding Your Course:

Think of words, thoughts, and deeds that block you from God. Write them in the margin. Say your own prayer asking God to remove them.

▼

Go, then, to all peoples everywhere and make them my disciples...
And I will be with you always.

— Matthew 28:19–20

A Yo-yo Helps

▼

Charting Your Course:

The children at church listened as the foreign missionary spoke. She said, "Living in another country is not always easy. When we first went to Brazil, the children even threw rocks at my children as they walked to school. We carried open umbrellas to protect ourselves. My children often cried and asked to come back to the United States.

"One day, our four-year-old son and I were walking under the umbrella. He had his brother's yo-yo. He was trying to learn how to make it work. We were laughing and talking. Suddenly one of the children who had been throwing rocks was under the umbrella with us. He was looking at the yo-yo. My son held out the yo-yo. I showed him how it worked. He laughed and laughed. Soon other children gathered around us. I told them that each day they could try the yo-yo, but they must not throw rocks.

"Each day my children would go out and let the Brazilian children play with the yo-yo. One day as they played with the yo-yo, my son showed the children a Bible story picture. He told the children about Jesus. Soon they were friends. We were even able to tell the children's parents about Jesus."

Exploring God's Word:

Throughout history, people have met together to worship God. This is a way to give encouragement to each other. You are a witness.

Old Testament (heritage): "Now, if you will obey me and keep my covenant, you will be my own people. The whole earth is mine, but you will be my chosen people" (Exodus 19:5).

The worship of many gods was common practice of those who lived near God's people. Often the Jews were tempted to follow their example. God wanted His people to remain true to Him. Worshiping together provided encouragement to remember their promise to God and His promise to them.

New Testament (example): "Many of the Samaritans in that town believed in Jesus because the woman had said, 'He told me everything I have ever done'" (John 4:39).

In Jesus' time, Samaritans were considered half-breeds. The "pure" Jews hated them. When the Assyrians invaded Palestine, they carried away the important people of Israel. The poor, feeble, and unimportant Israelites were left behind. The land was desolated and little remained. Other people were brought into the land to populate the area. These people intermarried with the remaining Israelites. They brought their own religions, mixing them with the Jewish teachings. Soon they became a mixed race and religion.

Normally the Jew would refuse to walk through Samaria. Jesus not only walked through their land, but stopped at a well for a drink. One way of worshiping is telling others what you know about Jesus.

Write down a person's name. Write down the way you will tell them about Jesus. Write the date you will tell them.

Holding Your Course:

Lord,
help me tell someone about You today.
Amen.

▼

Jesus grew both in body and in wisdom,
gaining favor with God and men.

— Luke 2:52

A Secret Choice

Charting Your Course:

Shane lay in bed thinking. She did not want to get up. Usually she liked to go to church, but today she did not feel like being with the others in her class. She was afraid someone was going to tell. She was almost sure that no one had seen her, but...what if they had?

"Come on, sleepy head. Get up!" Mother called. "We'll be late to Sunday School if we don't get going."

As Shane slowly entered her Sunday School class, Mr. Sands called to her, "Come on, we need you to help us."

At the table, Shane noticed a funny looking device. It had a balloon on it. On the table was a package of cigarettes. As the group worked, Shane saw the black stuff that collected inside the balloon as Mr. Sands blew the cigarette smoke into the balloon.

Later they talked about the reasons not to smoke and the reasons why some people smoke. Shane was very quiet.

As she sat in the worship center later, she thought about what Mr. Sands said. He had shown them a verse in the Bible that said her body was the body that Jesus lived in. She thought about the cigarette she had smoked. She did not feel good about what she had done, even though her parents would not fuss at her.

Suddenly she realized that she had her answer. Jesus had kept His body healthy. She could too. She knew Jesus would help her. Shane was glad she had come to church. She had the answer to her question.

Exploring God's Word:

Do you remember having good feelings when you were at church? Worship helps you face problems and troubles you have each day. As you worship you should remember God promises to be with you in everything you do, in whatever you say, and the places you go.

Old Testament (heritage): "Love the Lord your God, obey him and be faithful to him, and then you and your descendants will live long in the land that he promised to give your ancestors, Abraham, Isaac, and Jacob" (Deuteronomy 30:20).

The people of Israel knew God was a God of promises. They also discovered God did not go back on any of His promises. God wants you to remember as you worship Him that you have His Holy Spirit with you to help you live your life. He will help you with your questions.

New Testament (example): "On the third day they found him in the Temple, sitting with the Jewish teachers, listening to them and asking questions" (Luke 2:46).

The importance of worship was early recognized by Jesus. The strength and help that you receive as you worship will help you face whatever comes to you each day. Jesus knew the importance of listening and asking questions. He needed strength to live for God.

Holding Your Course:

Lord,
I do have questions about serving You.
It is not always easy to make the right choice.
Please help me.
Amen.

▼

You are my God, and I give you thanks;
I will proclaim your greatness.

— Psalm 118:28

My Special Worship Time

▼

Charting Your Course:

Have you discovered that worship is important for you as a Christian? Going to church *is* an important form of worship. Yet, worship can take place at other times and in other places. Remember: worship is showing praise, honor, and service to God. Worship is recognizing that God is real and that He is at work in your life.

Think about special feelings, special experiences, and special thoughts you have had as you worshipped. Where were you? In the space below, write your own story about a worship experience you have had. To help you write, be sure to include: where you were, what you were doing, whether you were alone or with others, and who you were with. Describe your thoughts and feelings. Describe the setting. Tell what caused you to think or do what you did.

Exploring God's Word:

Worship is special. Worship is personal. Only God is worthy of your worship. Worship is expressing your feelings about God.

Old Testament (heritage): "At the hour of the afternoon sacrifice the prophet Elijah approached the altar and prayed, 'O Lord, the God of Abraham, Isaac, and Jacob, prove now that you are the God of Israel and that I am your servant and have done all this at your command. Answer me, Lord, answer me, so that this people will know that you, the Lord, are God and that you are bringing them back to yourself'" (1 Kings 18:36–37).

Read the entire story of Elijah on Mount Carmel in 1 Kings 18:16–45. The pagan (not Christian) prophets had challenged Elijah's God to prove Himself. God knew at that time that the people needed a visible sign of His presence with Elijah.

The one difference was that the pagan god did not respond. Only *the* God works in those who have accepted Him as their Lord.

New Testament (example): "While he was talking, a shining cloud came over them, and a voice from the cloud said, 'This is my own dear Son, with whom I am pleased—listen to him!'" (Matthew 17:5).

Read the entire experience of Peter, James, and John on the mountain with Jesus in Matthew 17:1–13.

What an unusual worship experience Jesus and His three disciples had! Peter wanted to keep this special experience by building shelters on the mountain. Jesus told Peter He could not stay on the mountain, but He must go and tell others about Jesus.

Holding Your Course:

Lord,
I guess I have thought that worship was sitting in church.
I realize now that You are worthy of good thoughts, feelings, and actions from me. Thank You for being You.
Amen.

▼

Chapter Six

Jesus Teaches You to Give

▼

What's the first thing you thought of when you read this title? Was it money? If it was, then are you going to be surprised!

What does this little four-letter word *give* mean? Surprisingly enough this word has many dictionary meanings. Stop and look at several interesting ones: (1) to put into someone's hands; (2) to offer as a present; (3) to provide with, supply; (4) to pay as price; (5) to show; (6) to grant; (7) to volunteer; and (8) to sacrifice.

This chapter will challenge you to think about the ways in which you can give. Try out the new opportunities that are presented.

Turn in your Bible to Mark 12:41–44. This is a story about something Jesus observed. Take a few minutes to read about "The Widow's Offering." What does this story tell you about giving? Are you surprised at what Jesus had to say? How does Jesus compare the two groups of people? Use the rest of this page to draw a picture of the two scenes from this story. Pay close attention to details.

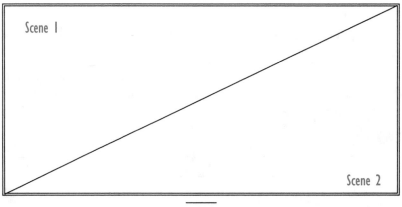

Scene 1

Scene 2

As Jesus sat near the Temple treasury, he watched the people as they dropped in their money. Many rich men dropped in a lot of money.
— Mark 12:41

Gift or Giver?

▼

Exploring God's Word:

Is it difficult for a rich man to give away his money? If all one is concerned with is how much he has then it would be hard for a rich man to give his money away. In looking at this verse from the passage, Jesus noticed that the rich men dropped a lot of money into the treasury box. The money they gave was needed. It is and was always needed so that the work of the church can go on. Pay close attention to what Jesus is really teaching. Is the gift as important as the giver?

Evaluate Your Position:

What kind of giver are you? What kind of gifts do you have to give? Is money the only way you can give?

Even though this story is about bringing an offering to the temple, it is talking about more than giving money. Write a prayer asking God to guide your thoughts and open your mind to new ideas about giving.

_____

_____

_____

Charting Your Course:

It's lots of fun to "hang out" on Friday nights at the mall. Molly and her friend Jill have just arrived. They see several other classmates as they enter near the food court.

Benny calls to Molly to come over and join him. He's sitting at a table with several others. There's lots of friendly fun going on when Jill sees their Sunday School teacher eating with her family. "Hey, Molly, there's Mrs. Thomas. Let's go over to say hello."

The two girls slip away from the group. Mrs. Thomas smiles when she sees them approaching. "Hi, girls!" she says. "What's going on with you two tonight?" Molly and Jill return the greeting as they pull up a chair and begin to talk. It's always fun seeing Mrs. Thomas. Both girls enjoy being in her class on Sunday.

As the girls leave, Mrs. Thomas reminds them that they need to bring money to buy the turkey for the Thanksgiving basket they are taking to a family next week. Molly looks at Jill as she says, "I really don't have any money to bring next Sunday. I spent all of my allowance on a new pair of jeans." Jill says, "Molly, your parents will give you some extra, then you will have something to give." "I'm afraid not," Molly says. "I have to make my allowance last all month. If I run out then I do without." Jill is really surprised because:

_____

_____

_____

_____

Holding Your Course:

Lord,
help me recognize when I have the opportunity to give to someone else.
Then help me know what I should give and to give willingly.
Amen.

▼

85

Then a poor widow came along and dropped in two little copper coins, worth about a penny.

— Mark 12:42

Pennies Count!

▼

Exploring God's Word:

What is meant by "a poor widow"? In that day a widow was a woman whose husband had died and left her with very few material resources (little money). This widow was poor. She had little hope of ever improving her circumstances.

Did her lack of hope or her lack of material resources (money) stop her from giving? The verse tells that she gave two little copper coins. What were these coins? What was their value? These coins were the smallest Jewish coins, *perutas*. They would be worth less than two cents today. This small gift caught Jesus' attention. Why was Jesus impressed with such a small gift?_____

_____

Evaluate Your Position:

Look back at the title of this section. These pennies that the widow gave were few in number. Their value was almost nothing. How could these pennies really count? Think about that for a few minutes. In the space by the pennies, write what, in your life, shows that you believe that pennies do indeed count. (Share your thoughts.)

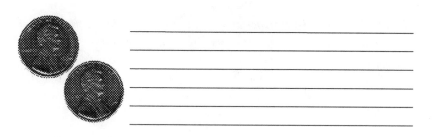

Which of your pennies will you give to help others?

Charting Your Course:

It was a hot summer day, and the wind was hardly blowing as Jenny waited on the porch for her ride to the pool. "Seems like I've been sitting here a long time," Jenny said out loud. Fifteen minutes more passed and Jenny was still waiting.

Suddenly she jumped up and yelled in the house, "Mom, Sue's here. I'll see you about four." Sue apologized for being late. "Mom got a phone call just as we were leaving."

After Sue's mom dropped the girls off at the pool, they walked up to the gate. Jenny couldn't find her money. Sue offered to pay her way in, but she didn't have enough money for both of them.

Jenny was really embarrassed and mad at herself. "I really appreciate your willingness to pay my way. I'm sorry I've ruined our afternoon together, but you go on in. I'm sure you'll find someone else you know. I'll just sit out here till your mom comes back."

Sue refused to go in. "We'll wait here together," she said. "You're my friend. I'd rather stay out here with you."

Holding Your Course:

Thank You,
God, for showing me that my pennies can make a difference.
Let my giving reflect the blessings You have shown me.
Amen.

▼

He called his disciples together and said to them, "I tell you that this poor widow put more in the offering box than all the others."
— Mark 12:43

Too Small to Count!

▼

Exploring God's Word:

Do you remember that Jesus said many rich men gave a lot of money. Then in verse 42, He said that the poor widow gave two little copper coins. Finally in verse 43, He says that the widow gave more than all the others. How could that be? Does that statement surprise you? What did He mean by that statement?

Evaluate Your Position:

It's hard for us today to understand how these two gifts could be compared. Jesus was always teaching when He talked to His disciples. He was also trying to teach you that no gift of love is too small to count. How do you feel about what you have to give? Have you ever thought that it was too small to count? Share your feelings about things you've given below.

_____

_____

_____

_____

Charting Your Course:

The following story will help you understand how even small gifts could help someone.

"This summer is really going to be awful," Mitch yelled at his mom. "It's not fair that we can't play baseball!"

"Mitch, I'm really sorry, but you know that my work schedule prevents me from helping. I'm sure that other parents are finding this to be a problem, too," Mitch's mom said.

"But, Mom, can't you just do something?" Mitch cried. For the last few years, it had been harder and harder to keep the little league program running. This summer there didn't seem to be enough interest to get the program started.

"Mitch, what do you think that I can do?" asked his mom.

"Why don't you phone some people to set up a meeting at our house tomorrow night? You could talk about what could be done," said Mitch. "Oh, I don't know! You know how tired I am at night," responded his mom. Mitch suggested she call another mom to help make the calls.

"I'll straighten things in the house and fix us sandwiches for supper," promised Mitch. "Please, Mom, please!" pleaded Mitch.

The calls were made and the meeting took place the next night. Mitch surprised his mom when he jumped up and called the meeting to order, "I know you are all very busy, but if everyone, including the kids, is willing to do something, can't we try to have a little league this year?" The group was surprised at Mitch and began to talk. Each offered to do a little. Before Mitch knew it the group had started making plans to solve the problem.

Holding Your Course:

Lord, help me to understand that no gift is too small
whether it is a gift of time or money.
Amen.

▼

"For the others put in what they had to spare of their riches."
— Mark 12:44

A Sacrifice!

▼

Exploring God's Word:

The rich men (others) gave only what they had to spare. What does it mean to give "what you have to spare"? Jesus was saying in this verse that the rich men would not miss what they were giving. It was not a sacrifice for them to give what they had just placed in the treasury box. This group of rich men had just given a lot of money, but they wouldn't miss what they gave.

Jesus called this to the attention of His disciples. He was teaching them about giving even when they didn't have a lot to give. If one's giving is measured by the sacrifice and not the amount, then what kind of giving did the rich men have? When you consider the need before you, think about the availability of resources for your use, then your giving is a sacrifice.

Evaluate Your Position:

The word *sacrifice* is not a word that most of us like to think about. I found that *sacrifice* means "to give up for the sake of something or someone else." Think about how sacrifice is reflected in your giving. On the graph, rate how much you're willing to give for the following reasons (A = parents, B = church, C = friends, D = a sick person, E = an elderly person, F = a stranger, G = a worthy cause. I = a little, 5 = a lot).

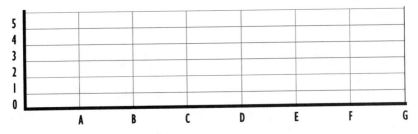

Charting Your Course:

It was 5:30 A.M.! Lucy crawled out of bed as Fluffy licked her face. There were no smiles for the dog this morning. Sleepily, Lucy opened the back door to let Fluffy out. She filled the water bowl and got out the food. Lucy thought, *I sure wish that dog didn't want out so early.* She loved her dog, but it was just too early in the morning.

"Scratch. Scratch." Sleepily Lucy found her way to the door. Fluffy's paws were all wet, but Lucy was too tired to do anything about them. Fluffy found the water and food as Lucy headed back to bed.

Just about the time that Lucy was back in bed and dozing, Fluffy jumped on the bed. "Go away, Fluffy. Leave me alone. I want to sleep." Lucy was trying not to wake her parents, so she once again crawled out of bed to take care of Fluffy.

It was now seven o'clock! Fluffy was ready for a nap. Lucy had to get ready for school. When Lucy came into the kitchen she found paw prints on the clean floor and dog food spilled. Quickly, Lucy cleaned up the mess.

Holding Your Course:

Lord,
help me feel good when I give up something for someone else.
Help me remember that You love a cheerful giver.
Amen.

▼

"But she, poor as she is, put in all she had—she gave all she had to live on."

— Mark 12:44

Giving Up!

Exploring God's Word:

What a contrast to the rich men who never missed what they gave. This woman gave everything! In her giving she was trusting that God would supply all her needs. Can you see how the offering this woman gave was a sacrifice? What made it a sacrifice?_____

_____

Jesus said that "she gave all she had to live on." Do you realize what that means? She did not have much to give, but when she finished, she had nothing. Wow! That's really hard to understand. Can you think of another person who gave all that He had?

Evaluate Your Position:

Do you feel that your giving could be considered a sacrifice? Make a list of three ways that you give. Then on the right side, next to each way, tell how your giving is or might become sacrificial. Once again remember that sacrificial giving is measured not by the amount given, but by the sacrifice.

	My Gift	My Sacrifice
1.	_____	_____
2.	_____	_____
3.	_____	_____

Charting Your Course:

School would be out in two weeks. Mrs. Jones knew it was time to quit her job. There was no one to take care of Beth and Steve. Every summer it was the same story. In the fall Mrs. Jones would have to once again search for work. Each year it got harder to give up her job and harder to find a new one. The worry over the loss of a job and less money was a concern. But the benefit for the family was the time Mrs. Jones spent with her children.

"I know that it is important to be at home, and I know I would only be making enough to pay for the child care, but I will miss working," said Mrs. Jones. "I've enjoyed getting out and being with people."

"I'm sorry that this happens every summer, but we both know it is best for the kids," responded Mr. Jones. "Until they are out of middle school, we'll have to do this."

Mrs. Jones nodded her head in agreement. She knew that for the next three years she wouldn't be able to settle into any kind of permanent job. "I'm willing to do this for our children," she continued. "I want them to feel safe and secure while they're at home during the summer. Too much can happen when an adult isn't around all day."

Mr. Jones smiled and said, "Thank you for making this sacrifice for all of us. The children are glad you will be home."

Holding Your Course:

Lord,
help me to remember that sacrifice is never easy,
whether it is money or something else that I am giving up.
Help me to remember the sacrifice Jesus gave for me.
Amen.

▼

"I tell you that this poor widow put more in the offering box than all the others. For the others put in what they had to spare of their riches; but she, poor as she is, put in all she had."

— Mark 12:43–44

Actions Speak Louder

▼

Exploring God's Word:

If the statement "actions speak louder than words" is true, then what do you think Jesus is saying about the widow's actions? Below is a list of possible meanings for this passage. Place a dollar sign ($) next to each one that is correct, and then mark through the ones that you think are not correct.

_____ 1. The widow's offering was a sacrifice.

_____ 2. Giving is the power of God's love working in one's life.

_____ 3. The amount of the gift was important.

_____ 4. No gift of love is too small.

_____ 5. In God's sight, the widow's gift was big.

_____ 6. The widow's love for God showed in her actions.

_____ 7. The widow still had something left.

_____ 8. The widow's stewardship was measured by her sacrifice.

_____ 9. The widow showed true devotion to God.

_____10. The widow committed her livelihood in trust to God.

You should have only marked through #3 and #7. Reread the list of things Jesus said about the widow's gift. How does your giving compare to the widow's? When were you last expected to give all?

Evaluate Your Position:

Think again about your actions in regard to giving. How do your actions measure against Jesus' teaching about giving?

Charting Your Course:

It was summer, and a new family was moving in across the street from Melissa. Melissa was very excited. The family had a daughter Melissa's age. She loved the idea of making a new friend.

As the moving van pulled up across the street, Melissa hurried to the front door. "Mom, hurry, let's go over to meet the new people," yelled Melissa as she ran out the door. Melissa was so excited, she was yelling and waving to the family like she already knew them. When the family's van stopped, Melissa was waiting for the door to open. "Hi, everyone, we're the Tates. I'm Melissa and this is my mom. Welcome!" To Melissa's surprise the back door of the van opened and a girl was sitting in a wheelchair, smiling. "Hi, I'm Sara," she said.

Melissa jumped in the van and excitedly began telling her all about the neighborhood, school, and church. "Why don't you come over and spend the day with me so we can get to know each other," Melissa asked.

Sara looked at her mom. "Oh, Mom, can I? That would be better than trying to stay out of everyone's way," Sara said. Melissa quickly spoke up, assuring Sara's mom that it was O.K. with her mom.

Sara's mom lowered the wheel chair down on a special platform as Melissa watched. "That looks like great fun," Melissa said. "I hope you'll tell me all about your special chair and why you're in it."

Holding Your Course:

Lord,
let my actions speaks so loud
that I don't have to tell anyone that I love You.
Amen.

▼

"She gave all she had to live on."
— Mark 12:44

The Gift that Counts Costs!

▼

Exploring God's Word:

It is hard to imagine how someone could give all they had to live on. We've already learned that she only had two copper coins, worth less than two cents. Why do you think Jesus made an example of her giving? Is Jesus saying that you should give all that you have to live on? Or, is He saying that you should be willing to give enough so that after you have given, you know it?

The Old Testament teaches to give a tithe, which is 10 percent of earnings. The New Testament teaches to give as God has given to you. How much is that? This New Testament story tells that the spirit in which you give is most important. If your spirit (attitude) is right, then you will know how much to give. You will give out of love and devotion to God, believing that He will provide for all your needs.

Evaluate Your Position:

Think about how you can give so that it costs you something. Is there something that you are saving your money to buy? Have you first taken your offering to church? Your offerings should be given before you use your money for other purposes. What can you as a young person give? Stop. Write down how much money you get. What do you think God expects of you? Discuss giving with your parent(s). Weekly Money Available: _____ Weekly Tithe: _____

Charting Your Course:

Sam was thinking about taking an offering to church. *Surely, God doesn't expect me to give him a dollar out of my ten-dollar allowance each week. That only leaves me nine dollars to do all the stuff I want to do.*

Sam thought about last Sunday. *Mr. Bill said something about being willing to give everything I have. I was surprised when he told us how much he gives. He said he believes that giving to God through our church must come first before paying bills or buying food.*

Sam rolled over on his stomach and picked up his Bible. "Let's see," Sam said out loud, "where is that passage we were talking about. Oh, I know, 2 Corinthians 9:7." Sam read the verse. "Each one should give, then, as he has decided, not with regret or out of a sense of duty; for God loves the one who gives gladly." Sam thought for a minute. *What I must do is decide what is right for me. Then I should give and be happy about giving it. That sounds too easy. If I decide to give ten cents and give it gladly, then is that all right?*

Another verse came to Sam's mind, but Sam couldn't remember where to find it. He thought for a minute. *The Bible tells us about how much Jesus gave when he died on the cross for our sins. That's why what I give is never as much as He's given me,* Mr. Bill had said. Sam decided, *I guess that maybe ten cents isn't enough when I think about it that way.*

Sam rolled onto his back and closed his eyes. He felt good about his decision.

Holding Your Course:

Lord,
help me to be a cheerful giver, one who is willing to give as You gave.
Amen.

▼

Chapter Seven

Jesus Teaches You to Trust the Holy Spirit

▼

In this chapter you will get to know the Holy Spirit. You have heard preachers and teachers talk about the Holy Spirit, but perhaps you've not given Him much thought. Often the Holy Spirit is referred to as "It." That is *not* correct. The Holy Spirit is "He." He is:

▲ The third person of the Trinity—God the Father, God the Son, and God the Holy Spirit.

▲ The person who exercises the power of the Father and Son in creation and redemption.

▲ The power by which believers come to Christ and see with new eyes of faith.

▲ The One through whom all else is seen in a new light.

▲ The power by which all Christians are brought to faith and are helped to understand their walk with God.

▲ The helper Jesus promised to His disciples.

▲ The One who glorifies Jesus and His teaching and works in the lives of individual believers and the church.

To help you begin to think of how the Holy Spirit helps you, find the following verses in your Bible. Match the phrase with the verse. Write the number which corresponds in the brackets.

1. Judges 3:10   [ ] Helps Christ speak through you.
2. Luke 4:1   [ ] Gives strength for extraordinary tasks.
3. Matthew 10:19–20   [ ] Helps us worship.
4. John 4:21–24   [ ] Is available to everyone.
5. Acts 2:16–21   [ ] Tests us.

(answers: 3/1/4/5/2)

Jesus stood up and commanded the wind, "Be quiet!" and he said to the waves, "Be still!" The wind died down, and there was a great calm.
— Mark 4:39

Afraid

▼

Charting Your Course:

Ben had worked hard. He had earned the right to compete as a member of the Bible Drill Team. Ben and the others on the team had practiced long hours. They had memorized page after page of Bible content.

Ben and the others were in a small room waiting. Suddenly Ben's legs began to shake. His hands became sweaty. He could hardly stand. His brain went numb, and he could not remember a thing he had learned. He felt tears stinging the back of his eyelids as he closed his eyes.

"Ben," Mrs. Allen said. "Come here." Hugging Ben, Mrs. Allen said, "I know you are afraid. Stand tall. Take a deep breath. This is only the church competition. You're going to do fine!"

Ben straightened up and breathed deep. He didn't feel very much better. He knew most of the people out there.

"Take your Bibles," Mrs. Allen told them. "We are going to practice some of the calls."

Before long, Ben was finding the books and verses. He was the first to step forward. He was not afraid.

Exploring God's Word:

Jesus teaches you to trust the Holy Spirit when you are afraid. In Mark 4:35–41, Jesus teaches His disciples what to do with fear.

After a very busy day, Jesus told His disciples to go with Him across the Sea of Galilee. Perhaps He thought they could be away from the crowds awhile. They would rest.

The Sea of Galilee is a freshwater lake, containing large amounts of fish. Sixty miles north of Jerusalem, the lake is thirteen miles long and eight miles wide at its widest point. The water is surrounded, except on the south, by steep cliffs and sharply rising mountains. When the cool winds rush down the mountains, they cause violent and unexpected storms.

Jesus did not worry. Some of His disciples were fishermen. They frequently fished on the Sea of Galilee. They knew about boats. They knew about the sudden storms. These were strong, brave men. So Jesus got a cushion and went to sleep.

Waking Jesus, the disciples were terrified of the storm. Jesus was not angry that they woke Him. He was disappointed they did not know how to handle their fear. Jesus spoke to the storm and to the disciples. Jesus reminded the disciples of faith. He reminded them that fear is handled by trust in the Holy Spirit, by faith in Him.

Evaluate Your Position:

Jesus did not fuss at His disciples for being afraid. He was disappointed with them that they did not know what to do with their fear. Fear is not bad. You are not bad if you are afraid. What you do with your fear or what you let your fear do to you is the question.

Holding Your Course:

Lord,
thank You for giving me the Holy Spirit to help me with my fears.
Amen.

▼

Peter was still trying to understand what the vision meant, when the Spirit said, "Listen! Three men are here looking for you. So get ready and go down, and do not hesitate to go with them, for I have sent them."

— Acts 10:19–20

The Decision

▼

Charting Your Course:

Mother and Daddy were unusually quiet at dinner. They frequently looked at one another. Caleb wondered what was wrong. Before he could ask, Dad said, "When we finish eating, I'd like for everyone to meet in the den. We need to make a family decision."

Caleb settled on the floor. Dad began talking. "You all know that we have been worried about Grandpa since Grandma died. He has gotten where he hardly eats and he falls easily. Mother and I feel that Grandpa is not safe alone any more. We think Grandpa would be better off living here."

Sitting up, Caleb said, "That's great. I like Grandpa. Where is he going to sleep?"

"That's what the family decision is," said Dad. "The only space we have is your room."

"Hey, wait a minute," Caleb said as he stood. "My room is small. Where will we put his stuff? Where do my toys go?"

"We will move the big bed out and put in the twin beds from Grandpa's. You would use the hall closet for your things. It would be tight, but we do not know what else to do," Mother explained.

"Caleb," Dad said, "it is your decision."

"I love Grandpa," Caleb said. "It will not be easy, but I will work hard to make it work for us."

Exploring God's Word:

Jesus teaches you to trust the Holy Spirit when you are asked to do something that is hard. In Acts 10:7–23, Peter was a Jew and Cornelius was a Gentile. Jews and Gentiles did not get along very well. To the Jew, a Gentile was a foreigner or stranger. To the Jew, Gentiles were thought to be heathen or pagan (people who did not believe in God).

Jews were forbidden to eat animals that chew the cud and do not have a split hoof. They were not to eat camels, rabbits, and hogs. Birds they could not eat were eagles, falcons, ravens, ostriches, sea gulls, hawks, vultures, storks, and herons. They were not to eat any creature from the water that did not have fins and scales. Gentiles could eat any of these.

What a dilemma! Peter was a Jew. In the dream he was told to eat this food. Then a Gentile sent for Peter. Jews did not go to Gentile homes. What did Peter do?

Evaluate Your Position:

Peter was asked to do something that was hard. Caleb was asked to do something hard. Jesus said that the Holy Spirit is with you when you have hard things to do.

Holding Your Course:

Lord,
thank You for Your Spirit who is always with me.
Today I have hard things to do. I am glad You are here.
Amen.
▼

We are witnesses of everything that he did in the land of Israel and in Jerusalem. Then they put him to death by nailing him to a cross. But God raised him from death three days later and caused him to appear, not to everyone, but only to the witnesses that God had already chosen, that is, to us who ate and drank with him after he rose from death.

— Acts 10:39–41

What Is Real?

▼

Charting Your Course:

Martha and her friends sat in the food court of the mall talking. Linda spoke. "I don't believe all that church stuff, do you? It can't be real!"

Kim answered, "Well, I don't go to church very much. We spend some weekends at Dad's. I like my class when we are there. We do neat things. Last time, I helped make a video about a guy named Peter. He didn't want to tell anyone of a different race about Jesus."

"Yeah, yeah," Linda interrupted. "Like I said, it is just a bunch of stories. How do you know it is real? Can't be!"

Martha said, "I have been listening and thinking. I've always gone to church. I never really thought about Jesus not being real. You have made me think."

"Well," said Linda, "you're the expert church goer! You tell us how to know that stuff is the truth?"

"Let's go to my house," said Martha. "I'll show you in my Bible. We just talked about it a couple of weeks ago."

Sprawled across her bed with her friends, Martha opened her Bible to Acts 10:34. She said, "Listen to what I read. When you hear the part that proves Peter knew Jesus was real say 'Stop.'"

Martha began to read. Suddenly Kim yelled, "Stop!"

"Wow, you almost broke my eardrum," Linda said. "What? Peter said he and others were witnesses of everything Jesus did. You cannot argue with a witness."

The girls talked about all they had heard and were told about Jesus. Linda said, "You know, Martha, if you don't care, I'll go with you and Kim to Sunday School tomorrow."

"Great!" said Martha. "Let's go ask Mom if you can stay the night, and then we can all go together."

Exploring God's Word:

People of that day had many gods. They added Jesus to their list of gods! Cornelius, an important and respected man, wanted the truth about Jesus. Peter had seen Jesus. Peter had heard Jesus. Cornelius heard about Peter and sent for him.

Evaluate Your Position:

The Holy Spirit helps you know the truth. The Holy Spirit gives understanding to those who listen. Truth is your best defense against doubts, questions, teasing, and disbelief. In the space below, write about a time you wondered what was real about God.

_____

_____

_____

_____

_____

Holding Your Course:

Lord,
it is hard for me to answer those who say You are not real.
Thank You for reminding me that Peter saw You.
Amen.

▼

My dear friends, do not believe all who claim to have the Spirit, but test them to find out if the spirit they have comes from God. For many false prophets have gone out everywhere. This is how you will be able to know whether it is God's Spirit; anyone who acknowledges that Jesus Christ came as a human being has the spirit who comes from God.

— I John 4:1–2

True or False?

▼

Charting Your Course:

Erin and Eric were twins. They liked having someone to play with and share secrets with.

One day while playing outside, several nice looking young men came into their yard. The men asked to see Erin's and Eric's parents. The twins told them their mom had gone next door. The young men sat down on the steps. They said they would wait.

The young men began telling the twins about their church and what it taught. Much of what they told was like what the twins did at their church. The young men showed the twins their Bible. On the cover, the twins saw a picture of someone other than Jesus. The young men quickly explained that this man had a vision from God. Their church tried to do all that the man told them.

Just then Mother came up. After listening to them for a few minutes, she asked the young men if they had accepted Jesus Christ as their personal Savior. The young men told her that Jesus was a good man, but they followed the teachings of another man. Mother talked to them a long time about Jesus. Sadly, the young men left. They did not believe what Mother said.

Mother and the twins talked about what the men said. Mother said, "You will hear of many who follow the teaching of men. You will hear them say that their person is right. You must remember to always ask: Does that person come from God? Jesus is the only one who is God's Son and had the responsibility to die for our sin. He alone could remove sin. Don't believe anything else, no matter how good it sounds."

Exploring God's Word:

In 1 John 4:1–6 Jesus teaches you to trust the Holy Spirit in recognizing cults (false teachers about God).

False teachers are those who falsely tell revelations (knowledge, news, disclosures) from God. They may worship false gods, serve idols, falsely claim to receive messages from the Lord, and wander from the truth, ceasing to be true teachers. The Bible passage you just read tells you to test what you hear and see against the fact: *Jesus is from God.*

Evaluate Your Position:

Know the true road to God. Many paths look right and look as though they will take you there. That is the way of false teachers or cults. Remember the "test" for the truth: *only Jesus is from God.*

In the space below, write down a situation you have faced at school, then write the wrong path to take and the right path to take.

_____

_____

_____

Holding Your Course:

Lord,
help me to be careful about what I see and hear about You.
Help me to always test it against Your truth.
Amen.

▼

Now listen to me, you that say, "Today or tomorrow we will travel to a certain city, where we will stay a year and go into business and make a lot of money." You don't even know what your life tomorrow will be! You are like a puff of smoke, which appears for a moment and then disappears. What you should say is this: "If the Lord is willing, we will live and do this or that," But now you are proud, and you boast; all such boasting is wrong. So then, the person who does not do the good he knows he should do is guilty of sin.

— James 4:13–17

The Best

▼

Charting Your Course:

"I can too!" Elizabeth shouted. "I am going to win the spelling contest and then I'm going to win the state contest. I am the best and I'll show you!"

Elizabeth and her friend Rebecca were at Elizabeth's house. They were studying for the spelling contest their class was having. Rebecca had not missed any words that Elizabeth had given her. Elizabeth had just missed two in a row. That is when Elizabeth shouted at Rebecca.

Rebecca said, "You're a bad sport. I'm not going to help you anymore. You are not a good friend." Rebecca began to gather her books and papers.

Mother saw Rebecca leave. "I thought you girls were studying for the spelling contest," she said to Elizabeth. "Aw, she thinks she is going to win the contest and I know I am going to. She's just mad 'cause I'm better," Elizabeth answered.

"You'd better be careful," Mother said. "Bragging is not a good thing to do. Remember what your Sunday School teacher told you?"

Elizabeth hung her head. She was remembering. Her teacher had said, "I know this is the week for your spelling contest. I want each of you to know that I will be praying for you. It is up to you to study hard and do your best. If it is God's will, He will allow one of you to win. I will be proud of every one of you. Now study hard."

"I guess I need to go see Rebecca," Elizabeth said as she slowly headed for the door.

Exploring God's Word:

Jesus teaches you to trust the Holy Spirit with your actions.

Why are you not to brag about what you are going to do? Underline the answer in James 4:13–17. When you ask God to take control of your life, He gives you the Holy Spirit to help you know what to do.

God's wants you to show self-control. Self-control is being in charge of your own actions.

Evaluate Your Position:

A key part of the Bible passage is verse 17 of James 4. Underline the verse in your Bible. God wants you to know when you give your life to Him, He provides each day for you. He gives you life.

We need to show self-control in all we do. We do not have to brag on ourselves when we do what God wants. Good comes from God. Begin a "God Gives Me Self-Control" (brag) list here:_____

_____

_____

_____

Holding Your Course:

Lord,
help me to control my actions.
I do want to be "in charge" of them.
I will begin by paying attention
to the things You do to help me to have control.
Amen.

▼

He preferred to suffer with God's people rather than to enjoy sin for a little while. He reckoned that to suffer scorn for the Messiah was worth far more than all the treasures of Egypt, for he kept his eyes on the future reward.

— Hebrews 11:25–26

The Choice

▼

Charting Your Course:

"You're a wimp, Beverly. Everybody is going to try it. I can't believe you won't. You're just a goody goody!" Angie said.

The girls were walking home from school. Angie was telling Beverly about the dope one of the boys was bringing to school. He had said he would let a group of them try one smoke if they met him in the vacant lot near the school.

"Angie, you heard what the policemen said at the school assembly. One smoke can cause all kind of problems for some people. It is not worth the risk to me. No, I am not going," Beverly answered.

"You don't understand," said Angie. "If you don't go, you will be left out of many things. Word will get around. You won't be invited to any of the neat parties. They will make fun of me for being your friend. Come on, please, Beverly!"

"No, I told you," Beverly said. "I decided last year that my body is very special. We studied how important it is to take care of your body while you are young. Many years after abusing your body, you can have trouble. I think too much of myself to do something that will cause harm now or later. No, I am not going to try drugs."

"Oh, I know. It is because you say you're a Christian," said Angie. "I go to church too. You won't go to hell just because you try one little smoke. Come on. If you're my friend, you will go with me."

Without talking the girls walked on. Beverly liked Angie very much. They had been friends all through school. They went to church together. Maybe Angie was right. Just one wouldn't hurt.

When they got to the corner where they went to their separate houses, Beverly said, "No, Angie. I won't try just one. God lives in my body. He would not like dope. I hope you won't do it either."

Exploring God's Word:

Jesus teaches you to trust the Holy Spirit in your choices.

Moses is an example from the Bible of someone who had many choices, just like you. If you read Hebrews 11:23–32 you will be reminded of some choices he had. Remember Moses could have lived well in the palace with his adopted mother, the Pharaoh's daughter.

Evaluate Your Position:

In Hebrews 11:23–32, underline the choices Moses could make. In the margin of your Bible, write the choice Moses made.

You need to make good choices because you are God's child. In the space below, write down good choices you can make that begin with the letters spelling "God's Child."

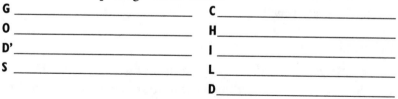

G _____   C _____
O _____   H _____
D' _____   I _____
S _____   L _____
                               D _____

Holding Your Course:

Lord,
help me to choose like You would.
Amen.

▼

"This, however, was bound to happen so that what is written in their Law may come true: 'They hated me for no reason at all.' The Helper will come—the Spirit, who reveals the truth about God and who comes from the Father. I will send him to you from the Father, and he will speak about me. And you, too, will speak about me, because you have been with me from the very beginning."

— John 15:25–27

Sad and Glad

Charting Your Course:

Jesus wanted His disciples to recognize the importance of the Holy Spirit. When Jesus died, He knew the disciples would need comfort. Jesus also knew the disciples would need help in understanding God's plans and purposes. The disciples would not have Jesus present to continue teaching them about God. Jesus had helped them with their daily choices and problems. Now the disciples would be alone. Jesus told them that God's love for them meant that He, Jesus, would have to die to be their Savior. God then would send to them the Holy Spirit to comfort, to help them make choices, and to help them with each day, in every way.

Exploring God's Word:

Jesus teaches you to trust the Holy Spirit to teach you about Him.

In John 15:25–27 underline the three things the Holy Spirit will do that Jesus had done for the disciples.

As you listen to your church leaders, do thoughts come to you that help you understand what is being said? When tempted to do things wrong, do thoughts come to you to remind you not to? Do you feel like you are not alone when afraid? Have you felt courage in making a difficult choice? Did you feel someone near when you had to do something hard? Do you know that Jesus and God are real? The Holy Spirit is at work.

Evaluate Your Position:

In this chapter you have discovered some of the many ways the Holy Spirit works. Think about how He works in your life.

Holding Your Course:

Lord,
thank You for giving me the Holy Spirit.
I like the way He helps me by bringing thoughts to me about You.
I like knowing He wants to help me.
Amen.

▼

Chapter Eight

Jesus Teaches You to Be a Friend

▼

Remember the words of the Golden Rule: "Do to others what you would have them do to you" (NIV). Consider how this verse applies to friendships. As you study Mark 2:1–12, you will be introduced to four friends and challenged to think about things that affect friendship.

Listed below are eight words that could be considered requirements (something that is needed) for friendship. Some of the words might surprise you. Match the words in the left column with the definitions on the right. Discuss your answers with a parent.

1. ingenious
2. demanding
3. persistent
4. concerned
5. unconventional
6. distinctive
7. active
8. joyous

a. causing happiness
b. out of the ordinary, unusual
c. constant effort or careful attention
d. involved in
e. original, imaginative
f. refusing to give up
g. worried interest
h. making a difference

Evaluate Your Position:

What things do *you* think are needed to have a friendship? On one of the journal pages in the back of the book, write the names of four of your friends. Then list under each what you think are the requirements needed for each friendship. As you work through this chapter you will be challenged to try these new requirements.

(Answers: 1=e, 2=c, 3=f, 4=g, 5=b, 6=h, 7=d, 8=a.)

Because of the crowd, however, they could not get the man to him.
So they made a hole in the roof right above the place where Jesus was.
When they had made an opening, they let the man down, lying on his
mat.

— Mark 2:4

Friendship Is Distinctive

▼

Exploring God's Word:

The special word in this session is *distinctive*. In Mark 2:1–12 four
friends are mentioned. What difference did they make?

The four friends were distinctive. Remember, *distinctive* means
"making a difference." The four friends did make a difference in the
life of the paralyzed man.

On the left side below, make a list of the ways the four friends
made a difference. On the right side, list ways you make a difference
in the lives of your friends.

1. _____ _____
2. _____ _____
3. _____ _____
4. _____ _____

What have you learned about being a distinctive friend?

Evaluate Your Position:

Write a short note to one of your friends telling him or her what you
have learned about being a distinctive friend.

Charting Your Course:

While playing one afternoon Amanda and Rebecca decided to bake cookies. Amanda's mom told them they could use her kitchen. Amanda thanked her mom and promised to clean up the mess.

The kind of cookie to bake was an easy decision. Both girls loved chocolate chocolate chip cookies. They checked the recipe and began to gather the ingredients. Amanda's mom had all but two of the ingredients. Rebecca called her mom and found what they needed. She quickly ran home to collect the items. As she hurried back she tripped and fell. The cup of sugar and the egg slipped from her hands.

Amanda was watching for her friend when she saw her fall. It only took Amanda a few seconds to reach Rebecca. Her knee was skinned and bleeding. Rebecca was mad. "Oh, Amanda, look what I've done!" she exclaimed. "It's no big deal," smiled Amanda as she helped Rebecca to her feet. They walked off laughing at the mess.

Back at Amanda's house, they first cleaned Rebecca's knee. When they finished they realized they didn't really want to bake cookies anymore. "It's a good thing we came to that decision together because we're still missing the two ingredients," laughed Rebecca.

The difference Rebecca made in the friendship: _____
_____
_____

The difference Amanda made in the friendship: _____
_____
_____

Holding Your Course:

Dear God,
help me to be a difference to those people with whom I am friends.
Amen.

▼

117

A few days later Jesus went back to Capernaum, and the news spread that he was at home. So many people came together that there was no room left, not even out in front of the door. Jesus was preaching the message to them when four men arrived, carrying a paralyzed man to Jesus.

— Mark 2:1–3

Friendship Is Concerned

▼

Exploring God's Word:

Read Mark 2:1–3 to answer the following questions.

▲ Jesus had gone back to: _____

▲ The news spread that He was back so many people came to the house where He was staying to hear _____

▲ The people must have been excited as they crowded closer so they could hear. The house was so full that the_____ carrying a _____ _____ could not get in the door.

Would you agree that the four friends were concerned? *Concern* is defined as "worried interest or being troubled about something." Do you see that the four friends were troubled about their paralyzed friend? They were so troubled or worried that they wanted to help him get to the One they believed could heal him.

Evaluate Your Position:

How do you show your concern for a friend? Take a few minutes to think of one friend that you are concerned about. What could you do to help that friend? Sketch a picture in the frame on the next page of the action or actions that show your concern for a friend.

Charting Your Course:

As a result of the Bible study, how would you tell a story? Use the facts listed and on the lines below tell their story.

Main Characters: Ben, Bobby, and Kevin

Time: Summer

Place: Swimming pool

Concern: Kevin's fear of the water

_____

_____

_____

_____

_____

_____

_____

Holding Your Course:

Dear God,
many times I am more concerned about what is happening to me
than about what is happening to my friends.
Forgive me and help me to be a better friend by showing I care.
Amen.

▼

So they made a hole in the roof right above the place where Jesus was.
— Mark 2:4

Friendship Is Active

▼

Exploring God's Word:

The study in this session centers on the ways the four friends were "active" in the paralyzed man's life. Look at verses 3 and 4, and notice the actions of the four friends.

Four men came, bringing to Jesus a paralytic hoping that He would heal their friend. Since they could not get him to Jesus because of the crowd, they made an opening in the roof above Jesus. After digging through the roof, they lowered the mat with the paralyzed man.

List the actions of the four friends:

_____

_____

_____

Because the four men cared about their friend, they were actively involved in his life. You probably won't be expected to physically *carry* a friend to another place, but you might help *bring* someone to Jesus. It might not be in the same sense that these friends did, but you could take a friend to church with you so he or she could learn about Jesus.

Evaluate Your Position:

For friendships to be strong, good friends must be active in the sense that they are involved in the other's life. Think about one friendship that is important to you. What makes that friendship strong?_____

_____

_____

Charting Your Course:

Tommy looked out the window of his dad's office. He noticed a man in a wheelchair waiting to cross the street. The light changed, and the man slowly rolled off the curb. He raised the front of his chair and eased down into the street. Before he could get across the street, the light changed. Traffic started, and the man worked hard to move the chair faster. Suddenly Tommy heard a loud "honk!" Then Tommy saw a guy run up behind the wheelchair. The smiling face quickly pushed the chair out of the street and onto the sidewalk.

Tommy thought about what he saw. Did the two men know each other? Were they friends? Why would someone risk his life like that? Tommy turned around to find his dad watching him. His dad had also seen what had happened. Tommy's dad explained that he had seen the two men together before. Surely they were good friends.

It is obvious that one man needed help and one had the ability to help. Think about the active role the smiling man played in the life of the man in the wheelchair. Did he make a difference? Today there are many people with handicaps who need friends. Is there someone to whom you could be an "active" friend?

Holding Your Course:

Dear God,
help me to find ways to be actively involved in the lives of my friends.
Also help me to follow through on those actions that I find I can do.
Amen.

▼

___

When they had made an opening, they let the man down, lying on his mat.

— Mark 2:4

Friendship Is Ingenious & Persistent

▼

Exploring God's Word:

Today we look at the words *ingenious* and *persistent*. The word *ingenious* means to be "original or imaginative." These men were not only ingenious, they were also persistent. The word *persistent* means they refused to give up.

In the story the four friends used their imagination and never stopped trying to get their friend to Jesus. The large crowd (v. 2) at the house could have prevented or even stopped the men from reaching Jesus. The fact that the man was paralyzed (v. 3) and couldn't walk might have kept the men from helping. The roof (v. 4) could have been a reason to give up. Lowering their friend down (v. 4) through the hole that they dug in the roof could have been a problem.

Evaluate Your Position:

Do you agree that the four friends were ingenious and persistent? Something wonderful happened to the paralyzed man because of the four friends. Remember what each word means in relation to friendship. Can you think of ways that you can be ingenious (imaginative) and persistent (never giving up) in your friendships?

Charting Your Course:

Read the following story as if *you* were the friend being helped. On the lines after the story share your feelings.

The summer sun was blazing hot as Tony walked out his back door. It was a great day for fishing. "Tony, I'm ready," yelled Tim from next door. "I'll be right over," Tony called back. Tony knew this would not be an easy day, but he wanted to take his friend fishing.

Tony got his fishing gear and headed to Tim's house. The fact that Tim had a broken leg would slow the boys down. "Hi," Tim shouted excitedly. "This is going to be fun!" Tony began to load Tim and their gear on the special cart he and his dad fixed up. The two boys started toward the creek. Tony knew that he would need help. He was already thinking about what he would do. Tim continued to talk excitedly about all the fish they would catch.

"Sure glad it hasn't rained in the last few days," said Tim. They both knew it would be tricky getting down to the water. Luckily, an older man arrived at the same time. He helped Tony guide the cart down the hill to the water. Both boys were thankful for the help.

Did you think about how Tim was feeling during the story? If not, read it again. Share your thoughts about how Tony was ingenious and persistent. What difference did it make to Tim's life?

_____

_____

_____

_____

Holding Your Course:

Dear Lord,
I've never really thought about how I could make a difference
in a friend's life.
Help me not to be selfish in my friendships and to never give up.
Amen.

▼

Because of the crowd, however, they could not get the man to him.
— Mark 2:4

Friendship Is Demanding

▼

Exploring God's Word:

The next word in this study of friendship is *demanding*. When something is demanding it requires careful attention or constant effort. Looking back at the story in Mark 2, you should find five things that needed careful attention. Unscramble the words below. Then check the answers to see how you did.

    1. dpeazryal anm _____ ___
    2. owh yhet dcearir imh ___ ____ _____ ____
    3. orfo ____
    4. dcwro_____
    5. woh heyt tel ihm wdno___ ____ ___ ___ ____

(paralyzed man, how they carried him, roof, crowd, how they let him down)

Evaluate Your Position:

Any one of these demands could have stopped the four men from getting their friend to Jesus. What demanding things might keep *you* from showing friendship? Write your friends' names on the next page. What kind of careful attention might you need to give each friendship? Is there some kind of constant effort that is needed? Beside each friend's name, list the demands each friendship places on you.

_____   _____
_____   _____
_____   _____

Charting Your Course:

Mia and Molly were nine-year-old twins. They lived across the street from their best friend, Sara. They enjoyed playing games, riding their bikes, talking on the phone, and hanging out together.

Molly loved to play tricks on her sister Mia. One time Molly hung upside down from a tree in Sara's yard. Then she started screaming while Mia was riding her bike down the big hill. It scared Mia so much that she almost ran off the curb. Another time Molly pretended that she had been hit by a car. She laid down on the side of the street and started yelling for Mia. Hardly a week went by that Molly didn't play some kind of trick. Each time Mia would scream, "Stop, or I'll get even with you!"

Sara was afraid of what might happen if Mia got mad enough to try to get even. Sara decided to talk to each girl separately. While talking to Molly, she reminded her that her tricks weren't funny and that they scared Mia. In talking with Mia, Sara tried to remind her that Molly really loved her and was just teasing. Sara hoped both girls knew that she cared about them. Sara encouraged them to talk to each other about their feelings.

List the demands on Sara. How did she show friendship?

_____
_____
_____

Holding Your Course:

> _Dear God,_
> _help me know that it isn't always easy to be a friend._
> _Help me not to give up just because I have to put forth extra effort._
> _Amen._

▼

So they made a hole in the roof right above the place where Jesus was.
— Mark 2:4

Friendship Is Unconventional

▼

Exploring God's Word:

Today's special word is *unconventional*. We said that this word means "out of the ordinary." It suggests something unusual. Think about this word in relation to the four friends in Mark 2. Did they have an unconventional friendship with the paralyzed man? Reread verses 1–4. How many people do you know who would go to such lengths to help someone else? The friendship was strong between the men because they were willing to be unconventional friends.

Evaluate Your Position:

In this session you will focus on how your friendships are unconventional. Sometimes a friend will need to be unconventional with you, or sometimes you may need to be unconventional with them. Below, write the names of your four friends once again. This time write something unconventional about your friendship beside each one.

1. _____   _____
2. _____   _____
3. _____   _____
4. _____   _____

Charting Your Course:

The following story is about an unusual friendship. After reading it, express your feelings about the story to someone else.

One day at school Jill's teacher talked about pen pals. She encouraged the class to pick a name and begin writing to them. Jill wanted more than anything to have a special friend that was all her own.

It didn't take Jill long. Even though they had never seen each other or played together, Jill had a new friend, Lucy. They were miles apart in different states. Each week the two girls exchanged letters. They shared about school, other friends, parents, and family. They even sent pictures of themselves and their families. It surprised Jill that she had gotten to know Lucy so quickly.

After writing to each other for more than a year, the girls began to make plans for Lucy to visit. Lucy checked the cost of airline tickets. They were too expensive. Lucy's visit wasn't working out.

Jill was very disappointed. She shared her disappointment with her mom.

Jill's mom decided to let Jill call Lucy. Lucy was also very disappointed. The girls made plans to start saving to pay for plane fare for one of them to visit the other the next summer. Jill was excited about the plans she had made with Lucy. It didn't seem to matter as much that the girls wouldn't see each other this summer. The visit could wait until next year.

Holding Your Course:

Dear God,
I want to be a good friend.
Help me to realize that sometimes I must do something unusual to
keep my friendships strong.
Amen.

▼

They were all completely amazed and praised God, saying, "We have never seen anything like this!"

— Mark 2:12

Friendship Is Joyous

Exploring God's Word:

The last word for this session is *joyous* which means "happy." See how the four friends brought happiness to the paralyzed man

Verse 5 says: "Seeing how much faith they had, Jesus said to the paralyzed man, My son, your sins are forgiven.'" Jesus recognized the faith of the four friends. He rewarded the paralyzed man, first by forgiving his sins. In verses 6–11, Jesus explained what He did for those watching. To prove He had forgiven the man's sins, Jesus then healed his paralysis. This proved that Jesus had authority on earth (v. 10). Look at verse 12: "While they all watched, the man got up, picked up his mat, and hurried away. They all praised God, saying, 'We have never seen anything like this!'" You can almost feel the happiness in the crowd as you read those words.

It is interesting that the four friends are not called by name, but their names weren't as important to this story as they were to the paralyzed man. He knew their names.

Evaluate Your Position:

What makes your friendships joyous? Again, write the names of four of your friends. This time write beside each what makes your friendships joyous or happy.

1. _____ _____
2. _____ _____
3. _____ _____
4. _____ _____

Charting Your Course:

In this final story you will write your own version of what happened after Jesus healed the paralyzed man. When you think about the story of the four friends, consider what is left out about the four friends. You can give them names and home towns. You might tell about the celebration they had after meeting Jesus. You might tell about how they praised God in some special way. This is your interpretation of what else might have happened.

Names of friends:

1) _____ 2) _____
3) _____ 4) _____

Name of paralyzed man: _____

Who fixed the hole in the roof? Where did the friends go after the healing? How did the four friends feel? What else did the man and his friends do?

_____
_____
_____
_____
_____

Holding Your Course:

Dear Lord,
I want my friendships to be happy.
Help me to do my part to make them that way.
Amen.

▼

Chapter Nine

Jesus Teaches You to Forgive

▼

Forgiveness can be defined as "to pardon, overlook, or excuse, an offender from the consequences of something." This chapter will examine forgiveness as an essential part of a happy Godlike life.

Sometimes you must show forgiveness for hurt that you have suffered. Sometimes you must receive forgiveness for hurt that you caused. No matter how hard you try to avoid both circumstances, they will happen in your life. This chapter will challenge you to think about the effects of forgiveness on your life.

Think about times when you have been involved in forgiveness. Each of these times could be considered a crossroad. On the crossroads below write what you remember about those times that would be helpful.

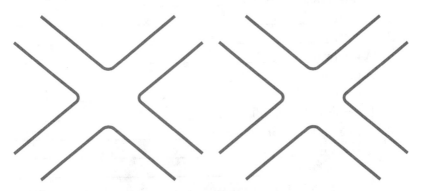

Our Bible passage for this chapter is found in Philemon. This one-chapter book in the New Testament comes right before Hebrews. It tells about a runaway slave who needed forgiveness. Read Paul's interesting letter to Philemon on Onesimus' behalf.

At one time he was of no use to you, but now he is useful both to you and to me. I am sending him back to you now, and with him goes my heart.

— Philemon 11–12

Character Traits

▼

Exploring God's Word:

Read Philemon 1–22. Notice how important forgiveness is to this story. In this session you'll do a background check on the main characters: Philemon, Onesimus, and the apostle Paul. Match the facts below by writing the appropriate character's name on the line.

1. A prominent Christian _____
2. A slave _____
3. A thief _____
4. A runaway _____
5. A prisoner in Rome _____
6. A member of the church at Colossae _____
7. Became a Christian in story _____
8. Wrote an IOU for the slave _____
9. The forgiver _____
10. The forgiven _____

Onesimus was a runaway slave which suggests that he may have stolen something. After meeting Paul, Onesimus became a Christian and wanted forgiveness from Philemon. Paul wrote his friend Philemon asking him to take Onesimus back and forgive him.

(Philemon—1, 6, 9; Onesimus—2,3,4,7,10; Paul—5,8,1)

Evaluate Your Position:

Do a background check on the person you know best—yourself! List the characteristics that show that you are:

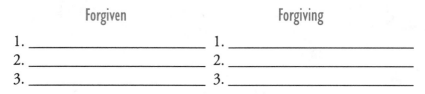

Forgiven   Forgiving

1. _____   1. _____
2. _____   2. _____
3. _____   3. _____

Charting Your Course:

Tony was one of the most popular guys in school. He played on the basketball team and was class president. He had always been a leader.

As Tony rode the bus home after school one day, he overheard two friends talking. One was telling how she had randomly dialed a number and made some silly calls. "I think that sounds like fun," chuckled Teresa. "Did you say anything or just wait until they answered and then hang up?" Julie giggled as she thought about how frustrated the lady had sounded, but she didn't tell Teresa. "Oh, I didn't say anything. I just kind of breathed heavy and then hung up."

"Since we're going to be alone at my house this afternoon, let's do some dialing," suggested Teresa. Julie smiled and then nodded her head in agreement.

Tony was curious about what he heard. He turned around in his seat and asked, "Hey, your little game sounds interesting. Can I join you?" The girls looked at him, giggled, and together said, "Sure!"

Holding Your Course:

Lord,
help me be careful how I let my character be molded. I know that
outside influences will all too often affect my decisions.
Amen.

▼

So I make a request to you on behalf of Onesimus, who is my own son in Christ; for while in prison I have become his spiritual father.

— Philemon 10

A Choice

▼

Exploring God's Word:

Reread Philemon 9–14. Onesimus was now a changed man. He had not only met Paul, the prisoner in Rome, but he had come to a saving knowledge of Jesus Christ. This created a desire in his heart to set things right with his master, Philemon. Verse 10 tells that Paul considered Onesimus his "own son in Christ." Paul was willing to write a letter to his friend Philemon on Onesimus' behalf.

At this point you see that because of the change (coming to know Jesus), the slave recognized what he had done wrong. He wanted to go back to his master. By returning he was taking a chance on losing his freedom entirely and maybe even being killed. Paul put pressure on Philemon to accept this man back as something other than a slave.

Evaluate Your Position:

Do you have a saving knowledge of Jesus? In the first chapter you learned about forgiveness in salvation. If you still have questions, please talk with your parents or a close friend. Think about how knowing Jesus has changed your life. Think about how knowing Jesus helps you forgive.

Charting Your Course:

Luckily for Tony he only lived a few houses from Julie. "I'll run home, leave my books, and be back in a few minutes. Wait for me!" he said.

Tony hurried in and called, "I'm home, where are you?" Tony and his mom exchanged greetings. "I hope it's okay to go over to Julie's this afternoon. I won't be late for dinner." Tony picked up a cookie and headed out the back door.

Teresa and Julie couldn't wait. They were already on the phone when he knocked. After several minutes, Tony knocked again, and then opened the door and stepped inside. *It's too quiet,* he thought. "Hey, where are you?" he yelled.

Julie and Teresa ran down the stairs laughing so hard they were almost in tears. Tony wanted to know what was so funny. Finally, Julie told Tony that they called the same number and got the same lady.

"You're kidding!" Tony was really surprised. "What happened?"

Julie started by telling how she remembered the number. Then Teresa told how upset the lady sounded when they said nothing.

"Now, it's your turn, Tony," giggled Julie.

"If she's upset, then maybe we shouldn't call her back so soon," Tony suggested.

Teresa and Julie began to tease Tony. Together they repeated, "Tony is a chicken! Tony is a chicken!"

Holding Your Course:

Lord,
it's hard to understand how easily I can be influenced to do wrong.
Help me to be strong.
Amen.

▼

If he has done you any wrong or owes you anything, charge it to my account.

— Philemon 18

Triangle Relationships

▼

Exploring God's Word:

Do you know what it means to say people are in "a triangle relation-ship"? The three men in this passage, Paul, Philemon, and Onesimus, were in that kind of situation. The need for each man to show love and forgiveness toward each other was what created the triangle.

Paul knew both men. He was trying to get Onesimus, the slave, to return to his master. Paul was asking Philemon, the master, to accept him back as something other than a slave. Paul's request was a hard one for Philemon. Paul was also willing to accept responsibility for Onesimus's debt. Interesting situation!

Evaluate Your Position:

Could you possibly be in a triangle relationship? Think about how you interact with others. It may not be as clearly defined as our story's triangle. On the lines below, write your name and the names of two others with whom you feel you have a triangle relationship.

▲ _____

▲ _____

▲ _____

On one of the journal pages in the back of the book, draw a triangle. Write your name on one of the points of the triangle and the names of your two friends at the other two points. Now write beside each name what will have to happen for forgiveness to take place.

Charting Your Course:

"Now, just wait a minute!" yelled Tony. "I don't think you're being fair." Both Julie and Teresa were surprised at Tony's strong reaction.

"It's only a silly phone call. What is the big deal?" Julie asked.

Tony looked worried as he tried to explain his uneasy feelings. "It sounded like fun when you were telling about it on the bus. I'm not sure we won't get in some kind of trouble."

Teresa really was amazed. "I thought you were Mr. Cool, Tony. Guess I was wrong."

Shaking his head, Tony said, "This isn't about being cool. It's about frightening someone. Do you have any idea who it is you are calling?"

Julie jumped up. "Who cares? Let's get a snack and go back upstairs. Tony, close the door as you leave."

Tony yelled, "I'm not leaving!" and flopped on the couch.

Stop. Draw a triangle. Write the three characters' names at each point. In the center, write what is needed for forgiveness to happen.

Holding Your Course:

Dear God,
I find it is unpleasant to be in a triangle relationship.
May forgiveness happen.
Amen.

It may be that Onesimus was away from you for a short time so that you might have him back for all time.

— Philemon 15

Righting Wrongs

▼

Exploring God's Word:

Roman law required Onesimus to return to his master to correct all his wrongs. His Christian conscience led Onesimus to return and ask for forgiveness for those same wrongs. The passage does not specifically state what these wrongs were, but being a runaway slave was a serious offense. Whatever the wrongs, they were upsetting enough for Paul to get involved. Read carefully verses 12–15 from a modern translation to see how serious Paul was about helping Onesimus.

Do you know of any laws that require people to correct their wrongs? Have you ever experienced a strong desire, Christian conscience, to seek forgiveness for wrongs that you have committed? Interestingly enough, all people too often find themselves doing things that are hurtful. Reflect for a few minutes about anything that might be bothering you. This just might be your Christian conscience telling you that you need to make right some wrong.

Evaluate Your Position:

How can you right a wrong? Now that you have spent time reflecting on what your conscience is telling you, what will you do about it? In the space below, outline a plan. Write three or four steps of how you will make the wrong right.

1. _____
2. _____
3. _____
4. _____

Charting Your Course:

Julie and Teresa couldn't believe Tony was acting so crazy, and Tony couldn't believe the girls thought this game was funny. None was willing to back down until after the phone rang. Let's listen in.

Ring! Ring! Julie jumped up quickly. "Hello."

"This is Mr. Johnson. I live down the street. I'd like to speak to one of your parents, please."

Julie felt funny. "I'm sorry. They aren't home. May I take a message?"

Mr. Johnson continued, "Yes, has someone at this number been making unnecessary phone calls this afternoon?"

Julie sat down hard. "What do you mean, unnecessary phone calls?" Then there was silence for a few seconds.

"Oh, I think you know what I mean. I want you to know that if another call comes to this number, I will call the police." Click!

Teresa ran across the room to find out why Julie looked so scared. "Who was on the phone?" Julie told about the conversation. "I can't believe he found my number. We only made a couple of calls today. I'm afraid we are in big trouble," Julie cried. "What will I do if my parents find out?"

Holding Your Course:

Dear Lord,
help me to stop and listen to my conscience,
knowing that it is You talking to me.
Amen.

▼

And now he is not just a slave… he is a dear brother in Christ.

— Philemon 16

A Gift

▼

Exploring God's Word:

Paul felt sure that his friend Philemon would forgive Onesimus. "And how much more he will mean to you, both as a slave and as a brother in the Lord! So if you think of me as your _____, welcome him back just as you would _____" (vv. 16–17).

In verse 18, Paul is willing to take on the slave's debt. "If he has done you any wrong or owes you anything, charge it to my account." Paul reminded Philemon that he owed his very self to Paul.

In verse 20 Paul asked Philemon, his brother, "Please do me this favor for the Lord's sake; as a _____ in _____, cheer me up!" Remember Paul was a prisoner in Rome, and though he was not in a jail with bars, he was being watched by guards. "I am sure, as I write this, that you will do what I ask—in fact I _____ that you will do even more" (v. 21).

Evaluate Your Position:

Have you ever been encouraged by one friend to forgive another friend? Do you think it was easy for Philemon to follow Paul's advice? Think about a time when you needed to forgive someone. It was probably not easy to take the steps needed. On the steps below write what a friend did to help you show forgiveness.

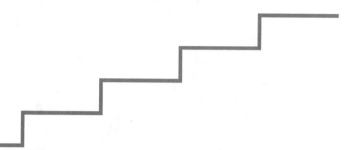

Charting Your Course:

Tony was still lying on the couch. "Now's your chance to show what you're made of. I know where Mr. Johnson lives. Let's go apologize."

Julie and Teresa could hardly believe their ears. "I don't think I can," answered Teresa. "It would really be hard." Julie stood up and said, "Mr. Johnson said he'd drop it if there were no more calls." Tony laughed, "How do you know someone won't accidentally call a wrong number and hang up when they realize it's the wrong number?"

A puzzled Julie asked Tony why he'd go with them. "You didn't make the calls—you aren't in any trouble."

Tony smiled at his friends. "I think it might make it easier if I went along. I know the Johnsons and they're really nice people."

Teresa was still puzzled. "Why would you help us when we were so mean to you?" Tony explained why he wanted to help them. "I hope that because I am forgiving you that it will be easy for you to forgive. Come on, let's go see Mr. Johnson. We'll all feel better."

Holding Your Course:

Lord,
help me to know that to receive Your forgiveness, I must always be
willing to forgive others the wrongs they do to me.
Amen.

▼

I am sending him back to you now, and with him goes my heart.
— Philemon 12

Changes

▼

Exploring God's Word:

After someone experiences forgiveness, he is changed! This passage doesn't tell how Onesimus acted after he was forgiven. Instead, look closely at what Paul told Philemon to expect from Onesimus. Paul related that Onesimus understood him when he said, "with him goes my heart."

In the next verse Paul said that he would like to keep Onesimus in Rome with him. Paul knew that for the gospel's sake, he would be of more help back with Philemon. The name, Onesimus, meant "useful or profitable." In verse 15, Paul suggested that Onesimus would now be able to live up to his name. In verse 16, Paul suggested that Onesimus would mean so much more to Philemon because he was now a "dear brother in Christ."

Forgiveness brings about change, not only of the person who is forgiven, but also the one who forgives. Both Philemon and Onesimus experienced change. Onesimus went back to his master a changed man because of God's forgiveness. After Philemon forgave Onesimus, their relationship changed. They were now brothers in Christ just like Paul and Onesimus.

Evaluate Your Position:

Think about someone with whom you have experienced forgiveness. What changes took place as a result? Write a prayer thanking God for His forgiveness and for the forgiveness you gave or were given.

_____

_____

_____

Charting Your Course:

The girls were reluctant to follow Tony. "What is the problem?" Tony asked. "I thought we agreed to go together." Julie hung her head and looked like she was about to cry. "I need to talk some more."

Tony suggested they sit at the kitchen table and list the pros and cons. Teresa got some paper and a pencil as Tony said, "We should first list the reasons why we should go. Then why we should not."

Tony could see Julie didn't want to go. "I hope you will do it, Julie. Forgiveness will make you feel better than living with a secret."

Tony smiled as Teresa began to talk. "Tony's right. I don't want to always be afraid that my parents or someone else will find out."

"Julie, what we did was childish and mean," Teresa continued. "I think it would be worse if we didn't accept responsibility for our actions. We should also tell our parents. Then we won't have to worry about them finding out and being disappointed."

Finally Julie agreed. She was now willing to meet the Johnsons and apologize. "I know we should go, but I'm just so embarrassed."

Holding Your Course:

Dear Lord,
help me to admit when I've done something wrong.
Help me to not use my embarrassment as an excuse.
Help me take responsibility for my actions.
Amen.

▼

May the grace of the Lord Jesus Christ be with you all.

—— Philemon 25

Joy

▼

Exploring God's Word:

In this story, God used Paul to bring two people together into a loving relationship of friendship and Christian brotherhood. Onesimus came to know and accept Christ as his Savior, and his life took on new meaning. God's forgiveness played a big part in this story.

Remember, one continually receives forgiveness and must continue to ask for forgiveness from God because of the sin that finds its way into his or her life. It is this forgiveness from God that requires you to be a forgiving person.

Evaluate Your Position:

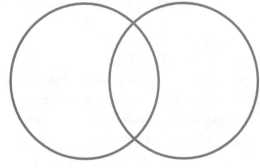

Draw two overlapping circles like those on the previous page. In the first, write things you have been forgiven for (actions, attitudes, etc.). In the second, write the feelings you remember having. In the overlapping area write what God gives when forgiveness happens.

Charting Your Course:

Knock. Knock.

"Mr. Johnson," Tony said. "Meet my friends, Julie and Teresa."

"Come in, Tony. It's nice to see you." Mr. Johnson introduced the three friends to his wife. "What brings you all over, Tony?" he asked. Tony looked at the girls. Before he could say anything Julie began, "Mrs. Johnson, I'm responsible for the phone calls. I'm sorry if I worried you. I promise that I won't do it again."

Teresa chimed in, "I'm sorry too. What we did was stupid." Julie added, "Also, Tony didn't make the calls. We are really embarrassed. We know better. Our parents will be very disappointed."

The Johnsons looked surprised. After a few moments Mrs. Johnson said, "Thank you for relieving my mind. I was afraid that someone might not be playing games. Yes, I was worried, but I feel better now." Mr. Johnson finished by thanking them for coming over. "I know this was not easy for you to do. The next time we get a strange call, we'll know that it's not any of you."

The three friends started home to talk to their parents. Julie smiled at Tony and said, "Thanks! You're quite a friend!" Teresa agreed as she returned the smile, "I'm not worried about my parents being mad. I just want to get this behind me." Julie agreed. As she said good-bye to her friends, she told them how much better she felt.

Holding Your Course:

Lord,
thank You for forgiving me of my sins. Help me remember the joy
forgiveness brings.
Amen.

▼

Chapter Ten

Jesus Teaches You to Help Others

▼

On the last trip you made, did you notice any people along the way that needed help? Perhaps you saw a car with its flashing lights on, or a person changing a flat tire, or someone just walking along the road. Did you wonder if they needed help?

In our day it could be very dangerous to stop along the way to offer help. In the newspaper and on TV, reports are given of those who have stopped to help and lost their lives. So just how can you practice Jesus' teaching of helping others and yet use good judgment about your own safety?

As you work through this chapter, you will have an opportunity to see some of the ways Jesus helped. Helpfulness begins with an attitude, then becomes a feeling of compassion, which results in using whatever one has available at the time to meet the need of someone else.

Evaluate Your Position:

As you continue your journey, think about your helpfulness. Just as you need to have a checklist before a trip, you need to occasionally have a helpfulness checklist. Use the one below as a beginning. Add to it other items as a result of studying this chapter.

My Helpfulness Checklist

[　] Attitude   [　] Feelings
[　] Willingness   [　] Useful
[　] Comfortable   [　] Resourceful

"Make certain you do not perform your religious duties in public so that people will see what you do. If you do these things publicly, you will not have any reward from your Father in heaven."

— Matthew 6:1

Helpful Friends

▼

Exploring God's Word:

Sometimes these verses are used as an excuse for not doing anything. Not everything that is done can be done in secret. So is Jesus saying that unless you keep it secret, you should not be helpful? Highlight the first line of verse 1 of Matthew 6 for the answer. Your attitude is the "secret way" of helpfulness. Though you may not always be able to keep your actions a secret, you can make sure your attitude is right.

Charting Your Course:

That night, the Lee family watched the weather forecast. Their friends lived where a storm was headed. As they watched nervously, they saw the main force would hit right where their friends lived.

"What can we do to help them?" Janice asked.

"Let's call them and tell them to come here right now!" four-year-old Edward said.

They laughed as Dad said, "We hope they have left already, but we will try to locate them to see how to help."

Nearly two weeks passed before the Lees were able to make contact with their friends. Their friends' house was damaged, and many things were soaked by the rain. Their friends needed to stay near their house. They were in a tent.

The Lees offered to bring their travel trailer to them to live in, as well as some other things that were needed.

Edward and Janice helped Mother and Daddy take many loads of food, linens, and clothes to the trailer. As the last things were loaded, Janice said, "Wait, I have something to send to Missy."

When Mother saw what Janice had, she said, "That is your very best and favorite game. I am proud of you, Janice, for giving your best."

Evaluate Your Position:

An attitude is a point of view, a feeling, or mood. It is easy to be helpful in a situation like the Lees faced. There are other situations when help is needed that an attitude of helpfulness would be difficult. There are times when you help and no one else knows. Think about your attitude of helpfulness as you read the Bible passage again. In the space below, write how you feel about being helpful. Describe your attitude:

_____

_____

_____

_____

_____

Holding Your Course:

Dear God,
I don't always want to help.
Keep reminding me of the help You give to me.
Help me to be more like You.
Amen.
▼

When Jesus heard the news about John, he left there in a boat and went to a lonely place by himself. The people heard about it, and so they left their towns and followed him by land. Jesus got out of the boat, and when he saw the large crowd, his heart was filled with pity for them, and he healed their sick.

— Matthew 14:13–14

Melissa Helps

▼

Exploring God's Word:

In Matthew 14:13–21, find the phrase that tells how Jesus felt when he saw a large crowd. Highlight the phrase. In the margin of your Bible write: Compassion=Helpfulness. Read the rest of the story to discover what else Jesus did for the crowd. When Jesus felt compassion, He put Himself in their place. Then He helped. List here the two helpful things Jesus did:

1. _____

2. _____

Charting Your Course:

Every day as Melissa rode the bus, she saw a lady sitting on the same bench. The lady was dirty and had a pile of bags with assorted things sticking out. As Melissa passed, the lady always looked up at the passing bus. Melissa felt as though the lady always looked at her.

One night at supper, Melissa told her mother about the lady. "I just feel so sorry for her," Melissa said.

Mother said there were so many who were out of work and who lived on the street. "Melissa, it's just impossible to help them all."

Melissa thought about the lady. She thought about what Mother had said. Still Melissa felt so sad when she thought of the lady. "What if that were me?" Melissa whispered. "I have to do something."

The next day, Melissa decided there was something she could do. In her mission group, the teacher had talked about the shelter for the homeless needing volunteers. They needed people to help in serving food. They needed people who would read to younger children. The mission teacher said that she would go one afternoon a week if there were those who wanted to go with her.

Melissa told her mother about the mission group needing volunteers. "You can go," Mother said. "I was wrong, there is something we can do."

Evaluate Your Position:

Jesus was teaching His followers that when people are in need, there is more that can be done than just feeling compassion. You need to give or do what will help. Sometimes we just think about the homeless or beggars as those in need. Look around you and seek ways you can be helpful. Write or draw a way you can be helpful every day of the week.

____Mon.____Tue.____Wed.____Thur.____Fri.____Sat.____Sun.____

Holding Your Course:

Dear God,
I've been thinking about being helpful.
Suddenly I find many ways I can help. Thank You for opening my eyes.
Amen.

▼

"At that time the Kingdom of heaven will be like this.
Once there was a man who was about to leave home on a trip;
he called his servants and put them in charge of his property.
He gave to each one according to his ability... Then he left on his trip."
— Matthew 25:14–15

The Dollar

▼

Exploring God's Word:

You need to read the rest of the story to find out what each man did with the talents of money the master gave. Read Matthew 25:14–30. The money (talents) was given to the servants according to their abilities. Each servant received no more or less than he could handle. Failure could only result if the servants were lazy or did not like their master.

The talents are the same as resources one has. A resource is anything you have available to you for your use. Some resources besides money are time, your mind, gifts, and information. List some others here:

_____

_____

_____

_____

_____

Remember, Jesus was teaching that all of you have resources and abilities. Jesus wants you each to use what you have to be helpful.

Charting Your Course:

Allison and her friend Leigh were walking home from school. They had an assignment. The teacher gave them each a dollar to use to help someone. They were then to write a report telling how they used the dollar. The child who increased the value of the dollar the most would not have to take the mid-term test.

At dinner Allison told her family what she had to do. They all had suggestions. Her brother said to put it in the bank and let it draw interest. Mom said to give it to a homeless person. Dad said to use the dollar to buy something she could use to make more money.

Allison lay awake a long time that night thinking. What could she do? Suddenly she remembered her teacher at church saying: "God wants you to work at things you enjoy. He has given you special abilities. Do those!" Then Allison knew what she would do.

The next day her legs shook as she knocked at Mrs. Kemp's door. "May I weed your flower bed?" Allison asked, when Mrs. Kemp answered the door. How did she use the dollar?

Evaluate Your Position:

Imagine you are Allison. Get a dollar bill. Write a picture story telling how you would use that dollar. You can use drawings for any words that can be pictured. Write your story on a journal page at the back of the book.

Holding Your Course:

Dear God,
I really don't have much to give to be helpful.
Help me think of a way to use what I have to be helpful.
I do want to help others.
Amen.

▼

"No! Love your enemies and do good to them; lend and expect nothing back. You will then have a great reward, and you will be sons of the Most High God. For he is good to the ungrateful and the wicked. Be merciful just as your Father is merciful."

— Luke 6:35–36

What's in It for Me?

▼

Exploring God's Way:

Help is an action word. One way to help is to take the initiative in meeting specific needs. Helping is easy when people obviously need help. Jesus teaches that real helpfulness means doing even for those you dislike or those who dislike you. The example Jesus used was giving a loan to someone that was disliked or known not to pay it back. Giving money should not be a high-interest loan that helps you, but a gift. You should give as giving to God. Giving shows your response to God as He continues to forgive you.

Charting Your Course:

The fifth and sixth grade class at church was studying what Jesus said about being helpful. They had decided that another word for help is *give*. One day they were talking about giving money to help. Their pastor had been preaching on tithing. Listen as they talked.

"I don't see any reason to tithe," Jason said. "If I want to help someone, I'll just give it to them."

"You'd better tithe," Alice said. "If you don't, you won't get anything given to you."

Stephanie said, "You heard Mr. Stephens say in his testimony how much he had gotten because he tithed. He drives a brand new Jeep!"

Mr. Ralph, their teacher, just listened. He let them talk.

"Besides that," José answered, "If you don't tithe, God will get you! That is right, isn't it, Mr. Ralph?"

"Get your Bibles. Let's see what God says about giving money as a way of helping," Mr. Ralph replied, laughing. "Find Luke 6:35 for the answer. Read the verse and think. Then tell me how Jesus said we should give money to help."

"Tithing is just a way to put more money together to help in bigger ways, isn't it?" said Jason.

"Have I ever been wrong?" Alice said. "Giving money is just one way to show God how grateful we are for what He gives to us."

"Yea, but Mr. Stephens still drives a new Jeep!" said Stephanie.

The class screamed out in laughter.

"If the worst person you can think of and someone you do not like asks you to borrow money to buy lunch tomorrow, what would you do?" asked Mr. Ralph. "That is the question Jesus asked about helping. You see, Jesus knows the importance we put on money. He wants us to give as though we are giving directly to God."

Evaluating Your Position:

How do you feel about giving money as a way to help? Write the headings below on a sheet of paper. Write how you feel about giving money to help. Also record what you plan to do to give as though giving to God.

Tithing * Help a Friend * Loan Money * Helping Someone I Don't Like

Holding Your Course:

Dear God, I often give so I can get. I am sorry.
I will give my tithe gladly.
Amen.

▼

155

Mary arrived where Jesus was, and as soon as she saw him, she fell at his feet. "Lord," she said, "if you had been here, my brother would not have died!" Jesus saw her weeping, and he saw how the people with her were weeping also; his heart was touched, and he was deeply moved. "Where have you buried him?" he asked them. "Come and see, Lord," they answered. Jesus wept.

— John 11:32–35

A Hug Helps

▼

Exploring God's Word:

Read John 11:1–44. In the story, highlight the names of Jesus' three friends.

Jesus visited these friends often. One time, Martha fussed because Mary did not help her with the meal preparation. Just before Jesus' death, Mary gave Jesus a precious gift of expensive perfume. Jesus loved these friends.

It was no surprise that these friends would call for Jesus when Lazarus died. Circle the words in the Bible passage that describe Jesus' feelings.

This story tells us how to be helpful when someone dies. Like Jesus, we can go to the family, feel sad for their loss, cry with them, and do whatever we are able to do. Notice how very little Jesus talked. Notice how much importance Mary and Martha placed on Jesus' being there.

Charting Your Course:

Joy saw that her mother's eyes were red. She had been crying.

"What is wrong?" Joy asked, running to her mother.

"My brother just called. Grandma died," Mother answered. "We must pack and be ready to go when Uncle Bill comes."

Joy hugged her mother as they cried together. They talked about the last time they had visited Grandma. They began laughing as they remembered Grandma carrying a ham which slid off the plate before she got it to the table.

Getting up, Joy said, "I'll get my things packed. I'll call Jeff to feed Happy while we are gone. What else can I do to help?"

Evaluate Your Position:

When someone we love dies, grief is a strong emotion. When people respond, it can be very helpful. Compare the way Jesus helped and the way Joy helped.

Jesus Helped By:

_____

_____

_____

_____

_____

Joy Helped By:

_____

_____

_____

_____

_____

I will help when someone loses a loved one by:_____

_____

_____

_____

_____

Holding Your Course:

Dear God:
I feel very uncomfortable when someone dies.
Thank You for showing me what to do.
Amen.

▼

He said to them, "Go throughout the whole world and preach the gospel to all mankind." After the Lord Jesus had talked with them, he was taken up to heaven and sat at the right side of God. The disciples went and preached everywhere, and the Lord worked with them and proved that their preaching was true by the miracles that were performed.

— Mark 16:15,19–20

A Secret Told

▼

Exploring God's Word:

After Jesus died and arose from the grave, He came back and visited His disciples. (Read Mark 16:14–20.) Jesus wanted to be sure that they knew and would tell that He was alive. "Go tell all the world that I have paid the penalty for sin," Jesus told His followers.

These followers had been forgiven of sin, had listened to Jesus' teaching, had watched as Jesus healed others, and had seen His death on the cross. Jesus was now asking them to help by telling what they had seen and heard. Every generation must tell the next generation about Jesus.

Charting Your Course:

Celese sat thinking. It bothered her that every time Jonell told a joke it was about sex or had curse words. Celese always felt awkward when hearing Jonell talk that way. Jonell was always willing to help Celese with her school work. What could Celese do? Would Jonell be angry if she was told about the jokes? What would help?

One day Celese and Jonell were at the mall. Celese said, "Jonell, I want to tell you about a friend who helps me with everything I do."

"Wow," Jonell replied. "You sure have been keeping him a secret. I want to meet him. He sounds great."

"Well," Celese began hesitantly, "He cares so much about me that He died for me. You see, Jonell, I used to want to do only what I wanted. I did not care about Him. I thought I could be good on my own. Then I found out why He died. It was because of sin. When I realized He was the only One who could make me good, I asked Him to take control of my life. Now He is with me always and is always there to help me. His name is Jesus."

Jonell sat quietly. "Why are you telling me this now? Why haven't you told me before?"

"I'm telling you now because I don't feel right when you tell jokes and use bad words," Celese answered. "I'm telling you because I realize how much He can help you, too. I am sorry I waited."

Evaluate Your Position:

Often we do not tell others about Jesus because we don't realize how much knowing Him would help them. List people you know who do not know Jesus. Beside their names list how knowing Jesus would help them. In front of their names, write a date that you will tell them about Jesus.

Date	Name	Jesus Will Help Them
_____	_____	_____
_____	_____	_____
_____	_____	_____

Holding Your Course:

Dear God,
why is it so hard to tell about You when You are such a good friend?
I want my friends to know You can help them
like You help me.
Amen.

▼

"And now I give you a new commandment: love one another. As I have loved you, so you must love one another. If you have love for one another, then everyone will know that you are my disciples."

— John 13:34–35

Help=Love

Exploring God's Way:

The Old Testament commanded people to love one another. So what is new about the command in John 13:34–35? Jesus is saying love is genuine when you love others as much as Christ loves you. Jesus is teaching that helping others is a way to show love. Look back through the chapter, and list the ways Jesus teaches you to help.

1. _____
2. _____
3. _____
4. _____
5. _____
6. _____

Charting Your Way:

"You're stupid!"

"Well! You're dumber than dirt!"

Their voices got louder and louder as they shouted insults at each other. Marty and Edward were only playing a game, but it was quickly getting out of hand.

"I think you two need to separate for an hour," Mom said as she entered the room. "You need to find something else to do. Go now!" Both boys looked at each other angrily as they got up.

Before thirty minutes had passed, each of the boys had asked Mother the time. Marty complained that he had nothing to do. Edward asked Mother for someone to come over. Mother said, "No." At the end of the hour, the boys were eager to play together.

Mother said, "One way Jesus said to be helpful is to show love."

Evaluate your Position:

Jesus taught that helpfulness is the same as love. He expects you to help as much as your resources will allow. Think about how *you* help. Do you match Jesus' teaching? In the following statements, circle your feelings about each with "1" being not strong and "5" being extremely strong.

A Helpful Way:

Do I have to?	1	2	3	4	5
Aw, let 'em do it themselves!	1	2	3	4	5
Here, I'll do that!	1	2	3	4	5
They did it. Let them get out of it.	1	2	3	4	5
I'll do it, but what's in it for me?	1	2	3	4	5
Can I tell you about my best friend?	1	2	3	4	5
I am sorry. I'll stay with you.	1	2	3	4	5
I feel sorry for them, but I can't help.	1	2	3	4	5
I'm going to get someone quick!	1	2	3	4	5
So? Not my problem!	1	2	3	4	5

Holding Your Course:

Dear God,
I want to be helpful. I feel Your love for me.
Thank You. Help me to show Your love for others.
Amen.

▼

Chapter Eleven

Jesus Teaches You
to Care for Your Body

▼

In this chapter you will study what Jesus teaches you about your body *and* the choices you make. When Jesus walked on the earth as a man, He felt and thought the same things you do. *What* He did with those thoughts and feelings is your example to follow. Jesus never said doing right is easy. To follow Jesus' examples will not always make you popular. But He does give you basic guidelines for living a happy life with the proper care of your body.

These guidelines are in the Bible. Remember your soul is "the stuff," the innermost, essence of life, your desires—the whole you. So in the Bible when you read *soul,* you need to remember it is the "real you." Jesus knew that for you to value your body, you must first value your soul. He wants you to give up self-centered determination to be in charge. He is teaching you that nothing is more valuable than your soul. He wants you to *choose* to follow Him rather than your wants.

You may struggle with your feelings and attitudes as you work through this chapter. You may encounter additional questions. Your church library may have resources that can provide additional information. Develop a friendship with a Christian adult (perhaps a parent) who provides a good role model for you. Talk with that adult about your feelings and questions.

Begin now to compare your desires and choices about your body with Jesus' teachings.

"The things that come out of the mouth come from the heart, and these are the things that make a person ritually unclean. For from his heart come the evil ideas which lead him to kill, commit adultery, and do other immoral things; to rob, lie, and slander others. These are the things that make a person unclean. But to eat without washing your hands as they say you should—this doesn't make a person unclean."

— Matthew 15:18–20

Pretty or Beautiful!

▼

Exploring God's Word:

The ceremonial washing of hands was of pride to the Jew. The washing called attention to the fact that the person kept Jewish laws. In the Bible passage, you hear Jesus stress that the "inner body" (what others can't see) matters most to God.

With all of the emphasis on health and exercise, many people work hard to keep their outward appearance attractive. Jesus is teaching that what is in the heart is more important. Jesus wants you to know at an early age: what is inside shows outside. God wants you not just to eat healthy food and to exercise, but to think healthy thoughts and have right motives. Jesus is teaching you to care for the inner body first.

Charting Your Course:

Whitney did not think she was pretty. She wore braces, and mixed with her freckles were those pesky pimples. When Whitney looked in the mirror, she didn't like what she saw.

Mom had just told Whitney that she was a beautiful person and that this was just a "stage" she was going through. They had argued about the amount of make-up Whitney was wearing. Whitney was tired of hearing that "beautiful person" stuff. Besides, she knew better!

Then several weird things happened to Whitney. There is just no other way of putting it—the happenings were just plain weird!

Mrs. Shoop, Whitney's English teacher, asked Whitney to stay after class. This was the same day Whitney's paper had been read to the class by Mrs. Shoop. She had bragged on the paper, so Whitney knew she was not in trouble.

"Whitney," Mrs. Shoop said. "I wanted to tell you how proud I am of you. Your paper is excellent, but I am more proud of the way you always use good English. You have a beautiful mind and you reflect it in your good use of language. I am proud of you. Please take care of your good mind because it adds to your beauty."

The second happening was at Whitney's locker. The cute boy with the locker next to hers seldom paid attention to Whitney. He had "those" pimples too, but Whitney did not mind. That same day, he looked at her and said, "I think you're kinda cute, and I've noticed that you're pretty smart too. Do you think you could help me study?"

Evaluate Your Position:

What are you like inside? What do you spend the most time thinking about? Read the passage again. Describe "the inner you."

_____

_____

_____

_____

_____

Holding Your Course:

Dear God,
help me to be beautiful inside and out.
Amen.

▼

He will be a great man in the Lord's sight.
He must not drink any wine or strong drink.
From his very birth he will be filled with the Holy Spirit.

— Luke 1:15

Just One!

▼

Exploring God's Word:

Luke 1:15 is telling of the birth of John, Jesus' cousin. As Jesus began His ministry, it would be John who would introduce Jesus. John was set apart for special service to God. The old Nazarite vow described in Numbers 6:1–8 forbade the drinking of wine because it was a vow of consecration to God.

In Ephesians 5:15–18, Paul is contrasting life filled with selfish desires with life filled with Christ's Spirit. Alcohol abuse is associated with producing a temporary "high." Paul wanted Christians to know that with the Holy Spirit, we have a lasting "high" because of the joy He gives. Alcohol clouds the mind and can lead to injustice and poor decisions. Jesus teaches you to care about lasting effects, rather than the immediate effects advertised about alcohol.

Charting Your Course:

Whitney had been helping Bradley each day after school. Both lived in the same apartment complex. Bradley's mom had died when he was young. He and his dad had lived there only two years.

Whitney noticed wine in the dining room cabinet and beer in the refrigerator. Whitney's family did not drink alcoholic drinks.

One afternoon Bradley got a beer from the refrigerator. He said, "Hey, how about one? My dad lets me drink one every now and then. He won't care."

Whitney did not want Bradley to not like her. She struggled with what to do. Her family had not talked about using alcohol. Still, Whitney felt it was wrong.

"Come on," Bradley said. "What are you waiting for? My dad says it helps him to forget and to feel good. Let's see if it does that for us! Besides, Mrs. Hinton, our housekeeper, is on the telephone. She can't hear us."

"No, " Whitney answered. "Alcohol doesn't help the body any. I don't even want to try alcohol of any kind. No thank you, Bradley."

Evaluate Your Position:

Jesus teaches that alcohol abuse does not show care for the body. Your body is God's creation. To abuse God's creation hurts God. Make a promise to God not to abuse alcohol.

My Promise

I, _____, on this _____day of _____, in the year of _____, do promise God to show care for my body by not using alcohol.

Holding Your Course:

Dear God,
I will remember my promise to You.
I ask You for the courage to keep this promise.
Amen.

▼

"The eyes are like a lamp for the body. If your eyes are sound, your whole body will be full of light; but if your eyes are no good, your body will be in darkness. So if the light in you is darkness, how terribly dark it will be!"

— Matthew 6:22–23

Watch Your Eyes

▼

Exploring God's Word:

The eyes are important to the functioning of the total body. Think of how the eyes affect the behavior of other body parts. Jesus is teaching you to take care of your eyes because what you see becomes a part of you. Seeing, wanting, getting, can consume your being and eventually your body. Jesus teaches that the eye can provide light for the body. It is your choice!

Charting Your Course:

Whitney was flipping channels on the TV when she saw the nude couples. She paused and looked guiltily around. She listened for her mother. Whitney felt uncomfortable watching the nude couples. She felt guilty. Quickly, she continued changing the channels.

Suddenly across the screen flashed her favorite TV actor. She stopped and watched. He was holding a package of cigarettes. He turned and lit the cigarette for a female actress. They were laughing and appeared to be having great fun. Whitney smiled as she changed channels.

Finally she found her favorite rerun. She settled in to watch.

As the commercial faded out, the face on the screen made Whitney gasp. The child hardly had a face. The eyes were the only part of the face recognizable. The child had been in an automobile accident. Her car had burned. She had barely escaped with her life.

The child was saying, "I am really lucky because I still have my eyes. They were not damaged."

Evaluate Your Position:

Think what you would do if you should lose your eyesight. What if you were allowed to see for only five minutes a day? What would you want to see? In the calendar below write what you would want to see for your five minutes each day. Remember that Jesus said that what you look at, you think about, and what you think about, you become.

Mon.	Tue.	Wed.	Thur.	Fri.	Sat.	Sun.

Holding Your Course:

God,
I look at so many things that cause me to desire the wrong things.
Help me keep my eyes on You.
Amen.

▼

We use it to give thanks to our Lord and Father and also to curse our fellow-man, who is created in the likeness of God. Words of thanksgiving and cursing pour out from the same mouth. My brothers, this should not happen!

— James 3:9–10

The Tongue

▼

Exploring God's Word:

Such a small part of the body—the tongue. But such an important body part! Jesus is teaching that the things you say and the things you don't say are both important. What you say reflects your beliefs, attitudes, and motives. Jesus is teaching you that when you use your tongue you reveal your true self—so be careful.

James recognized the importance of the tongue. He warns that the uncontrolled tongue can do terrible damage. Once words are spoken, they cannot be taken back. The contrast given between praise of God and cursing men points to the seriousness of the way you care for your tongue.

Uncontrolled tongues will gossip, put others down, brag, manipulate, exaggerate, complain, flatter, lie and teach falsely.

Charting Your Course:

Whitney cursed when the door slammed against her leg, causing her to stumble and hit her elbow. "I am coming!" she shouted angrily.

The family was in the car, waiting on Whitney.

"What took you so long?" Mother asked.

"You and your ironing board. Just as I passed the door, the ironing board fell. I stumbled and hit my elbow. Why can't you put your ironing board behind some other door? You sure don't let me keep my things behind the door," Whitney answered as she plopped into the car.

"That is enough, Whitney," Mother answered.

"Well, I'm right," said Whitney. "Most of the time I am right and you still don't appreciate me!"

"Whitney, let's have peace and quiet. We'll soon be at church," Mother replied.

Evaluating Your Position:

Underline in the story the ways Whitney allowed her tongue to be uncontrolled. What emotions from inside her are being expressed? Think about the way you use your tongue. Have you said things lately that you would like to take back? Have you had things said to you that have hurt you? Describe how you use your tongue and how you will be more aware of what you say.

_____

_____

_____

_____

_____

_____

Holding Your Course:

Such a little part of my body causes so much trouble!
I want to take care of my tongue
so that what comes out will be pleasing to You, God.
Amen.

▼

Some Pharisees asked Jesus when the Kingdom of God would come.
His answer was, "The Kingdom of God does not come in such a way
as to be seen. No one will say, 'Look, here it is!' or, 'There it is!';
because the Kingdom of God is within you."

— Luke 17:20–21

No More Pizza!

▼

Exploring God's Word:

Man has always wanted to know where God is. Jesus was teaching that each person who accepts God's forgiveness of sin and asks Him to take control of his life as Savior and Lord has Christ living in him. This is hard to understand. How is God in you? Because you know God is truth, you must accept the truth: He is in you.

Paul reminded the Christians in Corinth that their non-Christian neighbors were constantly watching. The way you live will show Christ or will not show Christ. Paul wanted the people to know that the care they showed toward their bodies would show the care they gave to Christ.

Charting Your Course:

"Can't you give me a pill that will just make them go away. It would sure be much easier."

Whitney and her Mom were at the dermatologist's office. He told Whitney she could improve her complexion by changing the food she ate. He was telling her to cut out as many greasy products as possible.

172

"But Doctor Dean," Whitney said. "That means pizza, fries, and all the good stuff."

"Now, now, Whitney," Doctor Dean soothed. "You can have them occasionally. Just remember that what goes in the mouth may pop out on the face. You have a wonderful body that is working hard, but it depends on you to put the right foods inside. It is your choice, Whitney."

Evaluate Your Position:

Start keeping a food diary. In the calendar below, record what you eat for a week. Decide whether or not you are taking good care of the "temple of God." On one of the journal pages at the back of the book, plan some "good food" menus. God trusts you to care for your body. It is your choice.

Mon.	Tue.	Wed.	Thur.	Fri.	Sat.	Sun.

Holding Your Course:

Dear Lord,
I do want to take care of my body by choosing good food.
Amen.

▼

"You have heard that it was said, 'Do not commit adultery.' But now I tell you; anyone who looks at a woman and wants to possess her is guilty of committing adultery with her in his heart."

— Matthew 5:27–28

Sex and You

▼

Exploring God's Word:

In today's world, sex is portrayed as right and great, if you don't get caught. From the beginning, God intended sex to occur only within marriage and for marriage to be a lifetime commitment. Jesus teaches that adultery can be committed with the eyes through lust.

Paul writes to the Corinthians that God gives us total freedom. We can do as we like. Then he writes, "But I am not going to let anything make me its slave. God did not give the body to rule us, but us to rule the body."

Outside of marriage, sex *always* hurts someone. It hurts God because it shows that the persons involved would rather do things their way than follow Him. It hurts others because it violates a commitment made to a relationship. It hurts you because it can bring disease into your body. It also hurts spiritually because it causes guilt.

Charting Your Course:

Mother told Whitney that one of her schoolmates had been diagnosed with HIV, the virus which leads to AIDS. Whitney was shocked. Whitney asked other questions about sex.

Mother said, "Sex was never intended to be wrong or ugly. God created sex for the pleasure of a man and woman married to one another. A result of sex was meant to be children who would be loved and taught to serve God. Anything short of that causes hurt."

"It really is confusing, you know," she said softly. "Everything we see and hear makes sex look and sound so right. Why?"

"Just always remember, Whitney, that sex within the marriage commitment is perfectly right and does not produce guilt. Anything else will," Mother said.

"I feel so many things when I see the loving way men and women act. I guess I would like to know someone loves me in a special way," Whitney responded.

"The Bible is our best guide," Mother said, reaching for hers. "Jesus taught that we must be careful what we see. To think about someone so much that you picture the sex act is the same as actually doing it. So Whitney, what we see does matter. I can only tell you that sex is completely right within the commitment of marriage, but completely wrong outside of marriage. You hurt God and yourself when you choose to do what you want, rather than what is right. God loves you so much, He gives you total freedom to choose. I hope you care about your body enough to choose to wait."

Evaluate Your Position:

It is not easy to keep oneself pure. The choice is yours!

Make a promise to God and to yourself to keep your body pure. I, _____, this _____ day of _____ (month), _____(year), promise to honor God with the body He gave me and keep it pure.

Holding Your Course:

Dear Lord,
I will remember to ask You to help me.
Amen.

▼

"Keep watch and pray that you will not fall into temptation. The spirit is willing, but the flesh is weak."

— Matthew 26:41

Mine, All Mine

▼

Exploring God's Word:

Jesus would soon die. He had taken His followers to a garden. These men were so special to Jesus. They had shared so much together. Jesus wanted to spend these last hours with them in prayer. Read the entire story in Matthew 26. Jesus asked them to stay awake and watch. Jesus was teaching them the importance of mental alertness. Jesus wanted them to realize that just "wanting to" is not enough. Mastery of your desires by allowing God to control them was what Jesus was teaching them.

Jesus' statement, "The spirit is willing, but the flesh is weak," related closely to the matter of temptation. Remember that the body and soul do not function apart from each other. The soul is the "true you." To love your soul is to care for your body. Jesus teaches you to care for your body; therefore, you must remain mentally alert lest you fall into temptation. Jesus wants to help you control your desires.

Charting Your Course:

"I don't see why I can't," Whitney said. "You just don't want me to have any fun."

Whitney slammed the door to her room. "She just doesn't understand what it is like to want to be thin," Whitney muttered to herself. "I wish I belonged to someone else!" she said, as she threw herself across her bed.

Mom and Whitney had been arguing again about Whitney's dieting. Whitney was taking diet pills. Her mother had just seen Whitney forcing herself to throw up. Mother had told Whitney that she was taking her to the doctor.

Who was right? Whitney just wanted to be thin like the advertisements in her favorite magazine. Did Mother care?

Evaluating Your Position:

In this chapter you have explored Jesus' teaching about your body. Jesus understands that growing up is difficult. He knows that the choices facing you are hard. He wants you to constantly be aware that temptation can happen in a variety of ways and situations. Jesus teaches you to be mentally alert—watch and pray.

You have also had the opportunity in this chapter to make promises to God. These are not easy promises to keep. Begin to cultivate the habit of pausing before making a decision. Ask God to help you to do what will honor Him.

Holding Your Course:

Dear Lord,
temptation is very real. I want to think before I choose.
I want to remember You are always present to help me.
Amen.

▼

Chapter Twelve

Jesus Teaches You
to Take Care of His World

▼

God is good. Everything He created is good. Each of us has been given the "special assignment" of taking care of God's creation.

> *Everything that God has created is good; nothing is to be rejected, but everything is to be received with a prayer of thanks.*
>
> — I Timothy 4:4

> *So God created human beings, making them to be like himself... "I am putting you in charge of the fish, the birds, and all the wild animals."*
>
> — Genesis 1:27–28

> *You appointed him ruler over everything you made; you placed him over all creation.*
>
> — Psalm 8:6

These passages tell of man's responsibility. Read Genesis 1:26–31 and David's song of praise in Psalm 8:3–9. In the space below, tell how these verses make you feel.

_____

_____

_____

_____

In this chapter you will explore ways to carry out God's assignment. You will then make a decision and do something. You will be the main character in each story even though the name will be different. It would be fun to make the activities in this chapter into family activities.

Instead, be concerned above everything else with the Kingdom of God and with what he requires of you.

— Matthew 6:33

School Project

▼

Exploring God's Word:

In Matthew 6:25–34, from the Sermon on the Mount, Jesus is teaching the people about not worrying. He is also teaching them that they should not let their worry keep them from doing what is required. Since God requires us to take care of His creation, why are things in such a mess?

Evaluate Your Position:

In the space below, make a list of the parts of God's creation that man has not done a good job of caring for:

1. _____ 4. _____
2. _____ 5. _____
3. _____ 6. _____

    Did you include animals, air, water, trees, the earth, and people in your list? Go back and evaluate what you wrote. What do you think life would be like without anyone of these?_____
_____
_____
_____

Charting Your Course:

Bobby's science teacher marched into class on the first day of the new school year with an interesting assignment. "Each person must choose a part of the school grounds to be responsible for during the first six weeks," said Mr. Wade. "Half of the six-week grade will come from this assignment."

It really didn't sound like such a big deal. Bobby knew immediately what area he wanted. Mr. Wade said, "I'm passing around a sign-up sheet. I've already chosen the areas that need the most attention." After they signed up, they went outside to look at their areas. Then they were to begin working on the project by writing their plans. Bobby was excited about this assignment.

Put yourself in Bobby's place. Treat this as your assignment. Think of an area around your school that needs attention. In the space below, develop your plans, and then put them to work.

_____

_____

_____

_____

_____

_____

Holding Your Course:

God,
thank You for this world that I have to live in.
Help me act responsibly.
Amen.

▼

"Look at the birds flying around: they do not plant seeds, gather a harvest and put it in barns; yet your Father in heaven takes care of them!"
— Matthew 6:26

Me? Do Something?

▼

Exploring God's Word:

The first thing listed in this passage is the birds. It almost sounds like Jesus is saying that these carefree creatures do nothing. That's not accurate. Close your eyes and imagine a bird as it flies around looking for food to eat and making a nest for its home. It knows where to go when it starts getting cold. Do birds really have it easy?

Other animals, too, are a part of this. God expects them to find food and shelter for themselves. These creatures play a big part in God's world.

The life cycle that God developed depends upon man's help. Birds and other animals are not helpless creatures, but they need to be protected. God expects you to do what you can.

Evaluate Your Position:

Does your community have leash laws? Does your state have laws governing hunters? How many birds can be shot during a hunting trip? Is a fisherman required to get a license?

Because you are responsible for taking care of this part of God's creation, tell what you know about what's happening today to birds

182

and other animals in your area. If you don't know anything about these laws, invite your parent to help you gather this helpful information. Check with your local Fish and Wildlife Office or the local Humane Society for helpful, up-to-date information.

Charting Your Course:

The newspaper headline read: "Dogs Run Wild!" As Chrissy's father read the article he grew angry. "Why can't people keep their dogs where they belong?" Chrissy asked her dad what the article was all about. He shared that the people in a certain neighborhood across town were having a problem with dogs roaming the streets.

"Is that the same place where the girl was attacked by the dog that tore a hole in the screen door to escape?" Chrissy asked.

"Yes, it is," her dad responded. "I really don't understand why people can't take care of their animals." It was obvious that Mr. Lawrence had very strong feelings about what was happening.

Chrissy continued to talk about the newspaper article. "Dad, if that problem was in our neighborhood, what would you do?" Mr. Lawrence looked surprised. "What do you mean, what would I do?"

Chrissy explained that she believed that people were responsible for the problem and also for solving it. "In Sunday School we've been studying about how we're suppose to take care of God's creation. What would you do to help solve this problem?"

Put yourself in the story. First discover if there is a place in your community that provides food and shelter for animals. Could you be a volunteer, or is their another way you could help take care of or protect animals? Share what you will do on a journal page.

Holding Your Course:

God,
thank You for birds, fish, and other animals.
Help me know how to care for and protect them.
Amen.

▼

"Look how the wild flowers grow…But I tell you that not even King Solomon with all his wealth had clothes as beautiful as one of these flowers."

— Matthew 6:28–29

Washed Away!

▼

Exploring God's Word:

God has made the earth very beautiful. Just go outside and look around at all His creations. The green grass that comes to life after the winter and the colorful flowers that bloom in the spring add to the beauty of our world. The leaves on the trees that change their color in the fall are also a beautiful part of creation.

In these verses Jesus is talking about more than the beauty of these flowers. He is reminding the people that God provides these things for man's enjoyment, but man is responsible for their care.

Evaluate Your Position:

If you live in a big city, it may be hard to see grass, trees, or flowers. If that is the case, you might want to suggest that the family take a ride. Together look at the beauty of God's world. If it is fall or winter, look closely for signs of God's beautiful creation. Wherever you live, go outside and enjoy God's world. Close your eyes. Smell. Feel. Think. Now look around you at what you just experienced. Share your thoughts by drawing a picture of this experience on one of the sheets in the back of the book.

Charting Your Course:

After several months of heavy rains, flooding caused big problems. The land, crops, and trees were destroyed. Many people lost their homes and everything in them. Many people came to help. They brought in food, clothes, and other supplies that were needed.

It was a big, big problem! All the help that came couldn't replace the trees, flowers, or soil that were washed away. The land had lost much of its natural beauty. It would take years for the trees to grow tall again. It would take a lot of time to rework the soil and make it usable.

If you lived in this flooded area, what could you do? As a family, talk about ways that your family could go about making a difference. What responsible action or actions could you take to help restore some of the beauty? Share your ideas in this space.

_____

_____

_____

_____

_____

_____

_____

_____

Now think of some place near you that needs this same kind of help (i.e., a neighborhood park, a community center, your church). Volunteer your family's time to help beautify that area.

Holding Your Course:

Lord,
thank You for providing this beautiful world for me to live in.
Help me to work actively to keep it beautiful.
Amen.

▼

Everything that God has created is good.
— I Timothy 4:4

Smoke Free!

▼

Exploring God's Word:

The word *create* means "to bring into being." Since God brought everything into being, He is the Creator. From reading this verse, you know that everything God created is good. This verse is not written in the past tense, *was*, but uses the present tense, *is*. What is the verse saying about God's creation, today? This part of the verse is leading you to think of creation in your present day as being just as good as it ever was. How do you think God might feel about the way man has taken care of His present day creation?

Evaluate Your Position:

Today, focus your thinking on the air you breathe. Much has been said about the air, the ozone layer, chemicals released into the air, and exhaust fumes from cars and smoke. What do you know about the harmful effects each of these could have on the quality of your life? Or on the lives of others? What, if anything, could you do to improve the quality of the air you breathe?

Do you know about any laws that have been passed by your local or state governments that deal with air quality? Share in a discussion with your family about air quality in your home and community. What has been done to improve it? What still needs to be done? How can you make a difference? Share any ideas or decisions your family has made because of this discussion.

Charting Your Course:

Tara's brother, Paul, was a teenager who had had problems with asthma most of his life. He had to be very careful when he was in public places. The family always had to be seated in the non-smoking section in a restaurant. Paul had to be careful not to get in a car with someone who was smoking. He also had to watch out for smokers at football or baseball games or other sporting events. There was always the problem of elevators or other closed areas where a person might enter just after putting out a cigarette.

The family had always made careful choices about what they did because of Paul's condition, so Tara was especially interested in helping educate others about the effects of secondhand smoke. Tara knew how hard her family worked to protect Paul.

Help Tara develop a plan that would teach those in her sixth grade class the importance of controlling smoke in the environment. Use the space below to share your ideas and/or your plan.

_____

_____

_____

_____

_____

Holding Your Course:

Lord,
it would be easy to ignore others' needs
when it is an inconvenience to me.
Please help me to be sensitive.
Amen.

▼

Nothing is to be rejected.
— 1 Timothy 4:4

Earth's Friends!

▼

Exploring God's Word:

The word *rejected* means "to throw away or discard." Think about this word *rejected* in relation to God's creation. This second part of the verse in 1 Timothy instructs you not to reject anything that God has made. The first question that comes to mind is, "What can be thrown away or discarded?"

Unfortunately, for too many years, man has chosen to live with a "throw away" attitude. There are problems with that. Many of God's natural resources are being used up too rapidly, and man has to change his attitude about how he is using God's creation.

Evaluate Your Position:

Much is being said about recycling. There are many programs—many places to take newspaper, aluminum and tin cans, certain types of plastics, glass, and cardboard. Most communities are doing a lot to educate their citizens. Schools teach about these programs and have started recycling programs. What do you know about programs in your community. If you don't know of any recycling programs in your area, decide how you and your family might start one.

Charting Your Course:

"Landfills Are Full!" "Too Much Garbage!" "Recycle Now!"

The headlines in most newspapers are a constant reminder of the importance of changing the way we live. Brad's mission group had decided to be a part of the solution, instead of continuing to be a part of the problem.

At their last meeting their leader raised several questions to help the group think about specific things they could do. First they identified what they thought was the problem. Bill thought the trash along the roadsides was an ugly problem. John wanted the group to set up a collection site for newspaper. The papers could then be sold and the money put back into the project. This would help recycle papers, plus allow the group to earn money. Joel thought they should get involved in setting up a recycling program at a retirement home. All the ideas were good.

All the suggestions that were raised helped the group discover that they would have to make a choice. Their manpower was limited and so was their time.

The group decided that the goal of the program was to show that they were friends of the earth. Troy excitedly suggested they call this project "Earth's Friends." The group liked the idea.

If you were a member of this group, what would you suggest? Write down your suggestions in your journal. Then get your family involved in starting some kind of project that shows you are truly Earth's friend.

Holding Your Course:

Thank You, God, for everything You have created.
Help me not to reject any part of Your creation
by treating it like it can be thrown away.
Amen.

▼

But everything is to be received with a prayer of thanks.

— 1 Timothy 4:4

Work＝Food?

▼

Exploring God's Word:

People are important to God's plan. People have caused most of the problems with God's creation. But without people, these same problems couldn't be solved. God wants us to be thankful for what was created. He also wants us to find solutions to the problems.

First Timothy 4:4 tells that God's creation should be received with a prayer of thanks. When was the last time you thanked God for the world that He created for you to live in? When was the last time you thanked God for other people that He created for you to know and live with in happiness? God really does expect each person to be thankful for and take care of His creation.

Evaluate Your Position:

What have you done lately that shows you are thankful for God's creation? Remember to think about everything God created. If you are truly thankful, you won't reject anything God created. Instead, you will find ways to take care of God's wonderful creation.

In the space on the next page, share what you think God expects of you in relation to the people part of His creation.

Charting Your Course:

Jeremy was traveling with his parents down the interstate. As they approached the stop on the exit ramp, Jeremy saw a man holding a sign.

"Will work for food!" Jeremy immediately called his parents' attention to the man. "Hey, look!" His dad assured him he had seen the man. "Well, what are you going to do?" Jeremy was surprised when his dad responded quickly, "Nothing!"

Jeremy's dad explained that many people choose this kind of a life instead of trying to find a steady job. Jeremy was really confused. He didn't understand how anyone would want to beg for food.

"Dad, I think we have a responsibility to offer to help this man." Jeremy's dad didn't agree. "I'm afraid we can't stop here and give him any kind of help. Usually these people only want a handout. They really don't want to work."

My guess is that most of you have seen someone holding a sign asking for work or money. Put yourself in Jeremy's place. What could you do to change his dad's mind about helping this person? This is a real problem. Many people are out of work or have lost their homes. What can we really do to help? Share your ideas. Then carry one out.

Holding Your Course:

There are so many people who need help, Lord.
Please use me.
Amen.

▼

"Our Lord and God! You are worthy to receive glory, honor, and power. For you created all things, and by your will they were given existence and life."

— Revelation 4:11

Special Assignment

▼

Exploring God's Word:

Revelation is the last book in the Bible. Revelation 4:11 should guide you to worship God. Notice three words from the passage: *glory, honor,* and *power. Glory* and *honor* both mean to show the utmost respect for. The word *power* means "to rule over or have control of."

God does deserve your ultimate respect and does have control over you from the standpoint that He is your Creator. Because God created you and gave you life, He should receive your praise.

Evaluate Your Position:

In this last session, you will be challenged to offer praise to God. Think about your list of things man has done a poor job caring for. What have you done during this study that shows you want to be a better caretaker of God's creation?

Write a prayer expressing your feelings about His creation:

_____

_____

_____

_____

Charting Your Course:

Your Special Assignment! Today you will have the opportunity to tell about anything you have done as a result of this chapter. Has your family started a project that is a direct result of sharing the information in this chapter? Use the rest of this page to tell how you have made taking care of God's world *your* special assignment.

_____

_____

_____

_____

_____

_____

_____

_____

_____

_____

_____

_____

_____

_____

_____

_____

_____

_____

_____

_____

Holding Your Course:

Dear Lord,
thank You for the job of caring for all of Your creation.
Help me to never lose sight of the importance of this wonderful gift.
Amen.

▼

Reuining you Relationship with God.
- You can lie to someone.
- Say Gods name in vain or something like that.
- Do something god doesn't want you to do.